HEGEL ON LOGIC AND RELIGION

SUNY Series in Hegelian Studies
William Desmond, editor

HEGEL ON LOGIC AND RELIGION
The Reasonableness of Christianity

John W. Burbidge

STATE UNIVERSITY OF NEW YORK PRESS

Published by
State University of New York Press, Albany

Printed in the United States of America

For information, address State University of New York
Press, State University Plaza, Albany, N.Y. 12246

Production by Dana Foote
Marketing by Theresa A. Swierzowski

Library of Congress Cataloging-in-Publication Data

Burbidge, John W., 1936–
      Hegel on logic and religion : the reasonableness of Christianity /
John W. Burbidge.
            p.   cm. — (SUNY series in Hegelian studies)
      Includes bibliographical references and index.
      ISBN 0–7914–1017–X (hard : alk. paper). — ISBN 0–7914–1018–8
(pbk. : alk. paper)
      1. Hegel, Georg Wilhelm Friedrich, 1770–1831—Religion. 2. Hegel,
Georg Wilhelm Friedrich, 1770–1831—Contributions in logic.
3. Christianity—Philosophy—History of doctrines—19th century.
I. Title. II. Series.
B2949.R3B87   1992
193—dc20
                                                                                    91–19111
                                                                                    CIP

10 9 8 7 6 5 4 3 2 1

For James and Mary

Contents

ACKNOWLEDGMENTS

This volume contains a number of independent articles, most of which have been published elsewhere. Chapters 2, 6, and 12 are reprinted from *The Owl of Minerva*, XXI, 2 (1990) 177–183, XVI, 1 (1984) 55–68, and XVIII, 1 (1986) 29–42. Chapter 3 was originally published in the *Revue Internationale de Philosophie*, XXXVI (1982) 111–124. Chapters 4, 5 and 13 started as papers read at meetings of the Hegel Society of America. The first is reprinted from *Essays in Hegel's Logic*, ed. G. di Giovanni (171–182) by permission of the State University of New York Press, © 1990 State University of New York Press; the second was first published in *Art and Logic in Hegel's Philosophy*, ed. Steinkraus, Schmitz, and O'Malley (New Jersey: Humanities, Sussex: Harvester, 1980) 201–218; the third, chapter 13, will appear in the proceedings of the 1990 meeting. Chapter 8 first appeared in *Dialogue*, XII (1973) 403–422; chapter 10 in *MOSAIC: A Journal for the Comparative Study of Literature and Ideas*, XI, 4 (Summer 1978) 67–80; and chapter 11 in *Philosophy and Phenomenological Research*, XLII (Dec. 1981) 183–196. A French version of chapter 9 was read at a Colloque sur l'égalité at the Université de Caen, France, and was published in *L'égalité, Cahiers de philosophie politique et juridique*, No. 8 (1985) 181–189. Thanks to the editors and publishers of the various pieces for permission to reprint.

Where possible, citations from Hegel are from G. W. F. Hegel, *Gesammelte Werke* (Hamburg: Meiner, 1968ff), and are identified by *HGW* and the volume number. Where material has not yet appeared in either that edition or the Meiner edition of the *Vorlesungen*, I have used the edition by H. Glockner: *Sämtliche Werke, Jubiläumsausgabe in zwanzig Bänden*, 4th ed. (Stuttgart: Fromann, 1968). *Enc.* and *GPR* refer to Hegel's *Enzyklopädie der philosophischen Wissenschaften im Grundrisse* (1830 edition) and *Grundlinien der Philosophie des Rechts* respectively. In both cases, rather than referring to a specific edition, I cite only the paragraph number, which is common to all editions.

I have used A. V. Miller's translations into English, identified by *Phen.* (*Phenomenology of Spirit* [Oxford: Clarendon, 1977]) and *SL* (*Hegel's Science of Logic* [Atlantic Highlands: Humanities, 1969]). In Chapter 10 I refer to J. B. Baillie's translation, *The Phenomenology of Mind* (London: Allen & Unwin, 1955) as Baillie. For the Encyclopedia texts, the English translations are found in three separate volumes. §§1–244 in *Hegel's Logic*, tr. W. Wallace and J. N. Findlay (Oxford: Oxford University Press, 1975); §§ 245–376 in *Hegel's Philosophy of Nature*, tr. A. V. Miller (Oxford: Oxford University Press, 1970); and §§377–577 in *Hegel's Philosophy of Mind*, tr. W. Wallace and A. V. Miller (Oxford: Oxford University Press, 1971).

Peterborough, Ontario
Good Friday, 1991

I

Lessing's Ditch: A Preface

In 1777 G. E. Lessing published a pamphlet with the title "On the Proof of the Spirit and of Power."[1] It is a commentary on a quotation from Origen, who argued for the truth of Christianity because of its "prodigious" miracles. Since reports of miracles are not themselves miracles, wrote Lessing, the reports are only as reliable as any historical account can ever be. In addition, historical truths cannot be demonstrated. Nevertheless Christian apologetics claim that "we must believe them as firmly as truths that have been demonstrated."[2]

This posed a problem for Lessing, since "accidental truths of history can never become the proof of necessary truths of reason." He fleshed this general statement out with examples:

If on historical grounds I have no objection to the statement that this Christ himself rose from the dead, must I therefore accept it as true that this risen Christ was the Son of God?

That the Christ, against whose resurrection I can raise no important objection, therefore declared himself to be the Son of God; that his disciples therefore believed him to be such; this I gladly believe from my heart. For these truths, as truths of one and the same class, follow quite naturally on one another.

But to jump with that historical truth to a quite different class of truths, and to demand of me that I should form all my metaphysical and moral ideas accordingly; to expect me to alter all my fundamental ideas of the nature of the Godhead because I cannot set any credible testimony against the resurrection of Christ: if that is not a *metabasis eis allo genos* [shift into another genus], then I do not know what Aristotle meant by this term.[3]

1

Lessing drove the point home with a vivid metaphor. "That, then, is the ugly, broad ditch which I cannot get across, however often and however earnestly I have tried to make the leap. If anyone can help me over it, let him do it, I beg him, I adjure him. He will deserve a divine reward from me."

In 1968, when I returned to university for graduate studies, Emil Fackenheim drew my attention to Lessing's ditch, and suggested I investigate the way in which Lessing's successors responded to that final plea. Kierkegaard had self-consciously adopted the image of an impossible leap, making it the central motif of his philosophical writings.[4] Schelling, in his lectures on modern philosophy, accused Hegel of an illegitimate move when he shifted from the logic to the philosophy of nature: "The point at which the Hegelian philosophy arrives in this move is a bad one, one which has not been foreseen at the beginning of the logic: an ugly broad ditch."[5]

Fackenheim suggested that Kierkegaard and Schelling were not alone in picking up Lessing's gauntlet, but that it motivated the religious philosophies of Kant, Schleiermacher, and Hegel as well. If I were looking for an interesting topic for a dissertation, this was it.

In the course of completing degree requirements, the range originally suggested was gradually narrowed, until the final submission focused simply on Hegel and the late lectures of Schelling.[6]

The papers collected in this volume reflect several aspects of that early preoccupation, now modified and elaborated. They reflect my conviction that Hegel's response to Lessing's challenge is of greater interest than that of Schelling (and, indeed, than those of Kant, Schleiermacher, and Kierkegaard).

Lessing distinguished between two classes of truths: truths believed on the basis of historical testimony, and the truths of reason by which we form all our metaphysical and moral ideas. The former are accidental and contingent; the latter are necessary and fundamental. The difference between them is so radical that it cannot be bridged.

Yet Hegel set out to provide such a bridge. And he did so by investigating both sides of the ditch—the eternal truths of reason as well as the contingent truths of nature and history.

By approaching Hegel from this perspective I noticed features of his logical discussion that are all too often overlooked. The truths of reason are not static: each one is involved in a transition into something else; concepts dialectically shift to their contrary. Yet they are not entirely fluid. Reason fixes opposites as alternatives; it recognizes that finitude is an inevitable counterpart to infinity, that contingency is the inverse of necessity, that universality becomes abstract and opposed to radical singularity. These concepts are understood both as distinct and determinate, and as complementary and interrelated.

On Hegel's Logic[7] offered some fragmentary results of that investigation into the nature of reason. An *exposition de texte* of the logic of actuality ("The Necessity of Contingency") was an early attempt to test the water, and became central to the demonstration that Hegel's logic was necessary. Subsequently I modified my original interpretation. The objective status of thought's dialectical becoming ("The First Chapter of Hegel's Larger *Logic*"), the tripartite scheme of transition, reflection, and disjunction ("Transition or Reflection"), and the central role understanding plays in the logical process ("Where is the Place of Understanding?") all received a more focused attention, both defending my interpretation against criticism and documenting some of its radical implications.

The conclusions reached are significant for Lessing's problem. According to Hegel, the necessary and universal truths of reason do not exclude the accidental, the singular, the finite, or the transitory as totally alien to its nature. Within the realm of pure reason, contingency and particularity—with all their diversity—are inevitable counterparts to, and conditions for, universal necessity. In addition, comprehensive thought posits and requires a contingency opposed to conditioned necessity, a finitude opposed to infinite regress, and a singularity opposed to abstract universality. Without that reference to radical difference, reason collapses into a simple identity that merely repeats its own inane formulae.

When compared with Schelling's alternative, the subtlety of Hegel's analysis becomes evident. For Schelling, reason moves from pure potentiality through pure actuality to a conjunction of potentiality and actuality: that pattern continually recurs, modified by its specific context. When nature and history confirm whether reason's projections are fulfilled, contingencies are to be ignored and only essential patterns brought to light ("Challenge to Hegel").

Reason may be open to contingent singularity. But that will not by itself resolve Lessing's problem. For, like Procrustes, we may use it to force external finitude into its own mold. Thus Schelling constructs an interpretation of Greek mythology and Christian revelation that makes them conform to the structure of potencies and potentialities. Hegel could well be guilty of the same sin. For he too incorporates the discoveries of natural science and the narratives of history into his systematic perspective.

After all, Hegel's reason does not leave contingency and singularity to persist as unresolved diversity. The logical discussions of these categories lead on dialectically to their counterparts until all are resolved into a more comprehensive unity. So contingency becomes but a component of absolute necessity, while singularity and abstract universality are coupled in judgement and finally integrated in disjunctive inference.

In a sophisticated move at the very end of his *Logic*, Hegel anticipates this challenge. In his chapter "The Absolute Idea," pure thought has come to terms with itself and has transparently identified its method. That self-transparency, however, reveals to thought its own limitations. All of the differences explored—the finite categories, the contingent transitions, the particularized alternatives—are nonetheless internally related as aspects of thought itself. Its infinite, necessary universality incorporates diversity into its own dynamic. That means, however, that it has had nothing to say about genuine diversity, about external relations, about actual contingencies in a world far removed from thought, about singular events that are not at all conceptual. Using its own categories. pure thought thus recognizes its own partiality. As a network of internal relations, it is outside of, and excluded from, all external relations.

Thought, however, does more. It can expect that whatever is other than thought can nevertheless be accurately described by some of the terms that have emerged within its own development. That "other" will constitute a realm that is contingent, transitory, finite, external, and singular (all of which are categories of the logic). So thought has, within its own vocabulary, concepts that will be appropriate to nature as its alien counterpart.

Thought anticipates something else as well. For reason can overreach its opposite and discover there a necessity inherent in the contingency, an infinite network of relations that sets the context for the finite, explanatory disjunctions that situate singulars. In fact, this is precisely what natural science and history have done, and continue to do, albeit in a disconnected way. They take contingencies in space and time and trace the connections that tie them together. The philosophies of nature and history reflect on this process, and set those segregated results within a more comprehensive perspective.

The achievement of pure thought, then, is appropriately two-sided. Thought has become self-consciously partial; on its own it can know nothing about external contingencies and historical accidents. To do justice to them it must take account of how they are different and unique. Nevertheless, it has tools for thinking about the ways they are different and for discovering how those differences are themselves related as components of identities, how singulars are integrated into generals, and how some contingencies relatively condition others.

So the second half of Hegel's response to Lessing concerns the ways we can legitimately talk about accidental truths. In other words, how accidents are appropriately transformed into truths in such a way that their inherent necessity becomes manifest and that reason is not merely instantiated but does justice to external differences and their significance.

The discussion of this aspect of the question is divided into two parts. The first considers some relations between thought and empirical reality in general: time as transition ("Concept and Time in Hegel") and political equality as logical diversity ("The Inequity of Equality"). The general principles involved are spelled out in "Is Hegel a Rationalist or an Empiricist?"

Hegel shows that even the most conservative description of natural and political phenomena can reveal an inherent rationality. The movement from future to present to past is an upside-down form of the logic of becoming. Political debates about equality falter because they ignore the logical point that similarities are abstracted from dissimilarities. By taking account of what we discover empirically and describing it accurately in the abstract categories of thought, and by noticing what happens when political dogmas are pushed to their limits, we find an implicit rationality that reflects, even though in an inverted form, the structures and patterns of the logic.

Lessing's dilemma, however, focused not on contingency in general but on the accidental truths of Christian history, which is the specific theme of the final section. For Hegel did not scruple in tackling that question directly. He showed how religious yearning itself seeks to overcome transience and change ("'Unhappy Consciousness' in Hegel"). Death, the final mark of human finitude, does not separate us from transcendent divinity, but is central to religious doctrine, feeling and practice ("God, Man, and Death"). The agony of the mystical dark night and the self-condemnation of confession, though religious truths, are the existential counterpart of rational negativity ("Is Hegel a Christian?"). In addition, when one abstracts the content of religious doctrine and practice from its determinate descriptions one finds a transition from individual to universal, a synthesis of particulars within a universal, and a universal that integrates singulars and particulars—three patterns that embody the logical forms of syllogistic inference ("The Syllogisms of Revealed Religion").

Thus the accidental truths of history show themselves to be the incarnation of the necessary truths reason unfolds. On the one hand, negativity constitutes the most profound moments of human experience; on the other hand three mediated movements are integrated into a single network of syllogisms. Indeed, this correspondence serves to establish the logic as true. Reason and Christian faith mutually justify each other.

Yet Hegel's achievement is not complete. Despite Lessing's explicit challenge, he does not show the necessity of Christ's resurrection. The individual God-man dies, and through death becomes universally present: the rational necessity of that can be recognized. But Hegel affirms no empty tomb, no resurrection of the body. He identifies instead with the traditions for which the resurrection is spiritual and the risen body is the Christian community. The reported miracle of the first Easter remains accidental, outside of the necessary truths of reason.

In addition, the fact that thought must be radically open to the contingencies of history raises a final question: when Hegel bridges the ditch between reason's necessity and history's contingency, is that itself an accidental and transient accomplishment or does it mark the final victory of pure thought? ("Is Hegel a Christian?")

While the various chapters in this volume originated as independent essays in response to particular conditions, they nonetheless reflect an inherent network of relations. Together they represent one effort to work through Hegel's response to Lessing's challenge. And in the course of doing so, they defend a number of crucial interpretative theses:

1. There is a significant difference between Hegel's logic and his philosophy of the real world. The "necessary truths" of the former can be developed within the confines of pure thought, abstracted from actual contingencies. The latter must be radically open to what in fact does occur, and to the contingent attempts by scientists and historians to understand and explain those events. While scientific and historical investigations inevitably use rational categories like "cause" and "purpose," they must do justice to accidental truths that could never have been anticipated.

2. The integration of conceptual thought and actuality, which Hegel calls the Idea, is not itself a simple feature of conceptual thought. It is thought overreaching that which is other than thought, an overreaching that must take account of the difference between concept and actuality—of the nasty, broad ditch—as well as their similarity.

3. Because the difference just mentioned is essential to the Idea, thought must continually be open. In other words, Hegel's philosophy is not closed to novelty but, in order to be consistent, expects its systematic comprehension to be temporary and transitory. New events will build on what has already been achieved. But that novelty will be as much rejection and destruction as elaboration and completion.

4. A final thesis is even more radical. The revision that will continue to be necessary in the philosophies of nature and of spirit reverts back to the realm of pure thought. For thought is an abstraction *from* reality, not an independent realm. As new differences and determinations emerge in reality, the logician will become aware of how thought has previously confused distinct logical operations and concepts, and how apparently disparate concepts are nonetheless dialectically related. While its method might be absolute, details of Hegel's *Logic* turn out not to be so.

Thus there is contingency even in the necessary truths of reason, just as there is necessity within the accidental truths of science, history and religion. The ditch is neither as broad, nor as ugly, as Lessing had made it out to be. The miraculous is not really as miraculous as it had appeared. That, however, leaves a final question for the reader to answer: Does Hegel merit the divine reward that Lessing offered anyone who would help him over the ditch?

LOGIC

The First Chapter of Hegel's Larger Logic

Discussions of Hegel's *Logic* often concentrate on the first chapter, which starts from pure being and ends with *Dasein* or 'a being' (improperly translated 'determinate being'). Quite regularly, commentators find the argument flawed. Having thus disposed of its foundation, they dismiss the rest of the logic as equally unreliable.

Thus Taylor comments: "But the derivation of Becoming here is not as solid as that of *Dasein*. This is the first, but not the last place in the *Logic* where Hegel will go beyond what is strictly established by his argument, because he sees in the relation of concepts a suggestion for his ontology."[1]

Similarly, Theunissen can only explain Hegel's move from 'becoming' to 'a being' by appealing to the "magic that converts it into being."[2]

Such criticisms are not new. And Hegel was himself aware of them. When he wrote the preface to the second edition, finished just a week before his death, he was able to reflect bitterly on the reactions it had generated so far:

A plastic discourse demands, too, a plastic receptivity and understanding on the part of the listener, but youths and men of such a temper who would calmly suppress *their own* reflections and opinions in which *original* thought is so impatient to manifest itself, listeners such as Plato feigned, who would attend only to the matter in hand, could have no place in a modern dialogue; still less could one count on readers of such a disposition. On the contrary, I have been only too often and too vehemently attacked by opponents who were incapable of making the simple reflection that their opinions and objections contain certain categories which are presuppositions and which themselves need to be criticized first before they are employed. Ignorance in this matter reaches incredible lengths; it is guilty of the fundamental misunderstanding, the uncouth and uneducated behaviour of taking a category which is under consideration for *something other* than the category itself. This ignorance is the less justifiable because this 'something other' consists of determinate thoughts and concepts, and in a system of logic these other categories must likewise have been assigned their own place and must themselves have been subjected to critical examination within the system. This ignorance is the most obvious in the great majority of the objections and attacks on the first Notions of logic, being, nothing and becoming which, itself a simple determination (the simplest analysis shows it to be so), contains the two other determinations as moments.[3]

The task of an interpreter is to follow Hegel's instructions and to develop "a plastic receptivity and understanding" so that we can appreciate the significance of what Hegel actually wrote.

Of crucial importance is the term "plastic." Hegel continually stresses that thought *moves,* and that the problem posed by the logic is to display the *movement* of pure thought. This poses particular problems for contemporary interpreters for, like Michael Inwood, they assume that "concepts and their interrelationships are static in a way that our thinking is not."[4] This radical difference in dynamic between the products of thought and the process of thinking reduces all of Hegel's descriptions of movement to nonsense.

In *On Hegel's Logic*[5] I attempted such a plastic approach, adopting from the *Encyclopedia* paragraphs 79 to 82 and the first preface to the *Logic*[6] the trichotomy of Understanding, Dialectical Reason and Speculative Reason. In that analysis, understanding starts by trying to fix pure being and then pure nothing. Each of these terms undergoes a dialectical transformation into its opposite. This double transformation then becomes the focus for speculative reason, which integrates them by means of the concept 'becoming' and then proceeds to articulate that integration.

This attempt to bring movement into the *Logic* has been regularly attacked by reviewers, for it relies on Hegel's psychology.[7] It is the movement of intelligence from one representation to another that becomes, once purged, the concepts of understanding and thought. But Frege and Husserl have claimed that such a psychologism builds on sand.[8] The transitions of intelligence are contingent and relative to individual subjects. They rely on chance associations which are idiosyncratic. As such, they cannot provide a solid foundation for all thought and all reality.

To the extent that I appealed to association, with its flavor of radical contingency and subjective relativism, the criticism is just. But that leaves unanswered the status of Hegel's plastic movement of thought. If that is not the transition that occurs in an individual subject's intelligence (or mind), what is it?

An answer to that question may begin with an appeal to our conventional term "implies." When one says, for example, that "a notion that is indeterminate is a notion that is empty,"[9] one has moved from the thought of indeterminacy to the thought of emptiness. When challenged we say that the first "implies" the second. We are not thereby simply appealing to our contingent associations. By using the language of implication, we are suggesting that the concept itself allows or requires a shift in meaning. Thought moves from one to the other. The initial concept did not remain a static atom, but became plastic.

What is the status of that movement? It certainly takes place in people's minds. But its validity does not depend on some chance happening in one intelligence or another. Its validity is something more objective and universal, constraining the individual psyche.

On Hegel's Logic provided a response to the charge of psychologism in its third chapter, "Problems of Language."[10] There, however, I concentrated on the universal sense or meaning of concepts; I did not expand the analysis to talk about the universal status of the transitions of thought. It can, however, be so extended. By making the transitions of thinking not just the arbitrary associations of an individual, but the distilled essence of what happens in the interaction of individuals and cultures, the subject of logical movement shifts from finite minds to the social reality of spirit.

While this analysis may be flawed, it at least provides a naturalistic explanation of the connections between ideas that logicians conventionally express by the word *implication*. And it allows a movement from meaning to meaning as part of the significance of conceptual thought. Those, like Inwood, who stipulate a priori that concepts are static and immovable fail to notice that it is belied by their own practice when they draw out the implications of a particular thesis.

The claim that conceptual or logical thought involves a movement of intelligence, refined through social interaction, does justice, then, to the actual operations of thinking in a way that conventional discussions of logic do not.

There is, however, another of Hegel's subtle maneuvres that is not captured by the analysis in *On Hegel's Logic*.

In the first paragraph under "Becoming," Hegel has two distinct descriptions of the truth.[11] First, pure being and pure nothing is the same; each one has already passed over into the other. Second, they are not the same but absolutely different, so that each has disappeared into its opposite. In *On Hegel's Logic* the crucial move is the first—the passing over; it becomes the ground of 'becoming', noticed only after it has already passed. But that fails to take seriously the initial sentence: pure being and pure nothing is the same. The singular verb reinforces the content of the sentence to suggest that there is not movement at all, but simply a single identity. This by itself cannot generate the concept 'becoming'. Only when the moment of identity is combined with the moment of nonidentity does 'becoming' make its appearance—only when the moment of passing over is combined with the moment of disappearance.

But from what does this second moment of difference and disappearance arise? The first two paragraphs of the chapter describe the passing over from one to the other: they attempt to display in language the movement of implication.[12]

What those paragraphs do not describe, but what they presuppose, is the absolute difference of being and nothing. The second "truth" in the paragraph on "Unity of Being and Nothing" is not the result, posited by the earlier dialectical movement, but the presupposition upon which it was based.[13] The critical movement, then, is not from being to nothing or from nothing to being, but from their absolute difference to their complete identity. The difference disappears.

However, there is something else that 'becoming' requires. It is not simply that one starts from difference and ends up with identity. It is that both moments are necessary. The movement can only be understood as movement when both presupposition and posited result, even though contradictory, are held together at the same time. Then it is recognized as a "movement in which both are differentiated, but through a difference, which just as immediately dissolved itself."[14] 'Becoming' is the ground that explains the contradiction. It is the universal.

In the preface to the first edition, Hegel describes positive reason as that which generates the universal *and conceives the particular in it*.[15] Hegel calls the process of particularizing a universal the work of understanding.[16] Once reflection has established the ground of the contradiction as 'becoming', understanding returns in a new guise to render that general concept determinate.

That process of rendering terms precise is spelled out in the second paragraph of the section on becoming: "Moments of Becoming: Coming-to-be and Ceasing-to-be."[17] It refines and defines the various constituents of the general concept. To do so, it considers the whole concept, the nonidentity as well as the identity; it abstracts from neither.

Once again thought is working out implications. This time, however, it is not a simple movement from one to another. Nor is it the reflective recognition of the difference between presupposition and posited (or implied) result. It is the articulation of the constituent moments of a complex thought, rendering them determinate and fixed. It is the inferential act of analysis.

In becoming, being and nothing are not simply identical. One starts as being and passes over (or disappears) into nothing; the other starts as nothing and passes over (or disappears) into being. There are, then, two distinct terms, and two distinct processes. These two kinds of becoming are two particulars under one universal. They are disjuncts. Becoming is *both* coming to be *and* ceasing to be; it is *either* one *or* the other.[18]

The two particulars, however, are not simply disjuncts. They are opposites. The precision of conceiving particulars has led to a complex universal that is totally described in an exclusive disjunction. Both particulars make up the universal; but each excludes the other. They constitute an exclusive 'either/or'.

Yet the exclusion is not absolute. For they are two processes or movements, and the end of one establishes the presupposition of the other. They imply each other. The movement is a single complex whole. The two particulars are conjoined into a tight 'both/and'.

At this point Hegel makes the critical logical move.

In the natural order, particulars are simply external to each other. In formal logic, external reflection defines radical opposites as contradictories. But when thought is acknowledged to be not simply concepts but implications—the movement from concept to concept—then a new possibility opens. For one movement can move into its successor and they can become a single movement. And if that single movement is a circle, returning to its origin, then it can collapse into a point. The tension that generated it dissolves into a peaceful unity.[19]

It is this character of pure thinking that enables an immediate unity to result from a mediating process. For here understanding fixes on the resulting unity and ignores the process by which it is generated. It allows the movement of disappearing to disappear. And a new concept emerges: 'a being'.

How and why does this occur? Because the three rational operations of understanding, dialectic and speculative reason[20] are reapplied at a second order of complexity: at the level of the universal ground or concept of becoming. Understanding defines its disjuncts. Dialectic reaffirms their mutual implication. Positive reason recognizes their integration as a quiescent unity.

The first use of the three operations—from pure being and pure nothing through their passing over/disappearance to becoming—occurs as a movement of simple implication, of simple becoming. It is basically dialectical. The second use of the three operations—from individuating the disjuncts through their mutual implication to their unity—occurs as determinate moments of a reflective unity; at each stage thought compares both what it posits and what it presupposes. At this stage thought is speculative.

But there might be a third use as well: the three operations recursively function under the aegis of conceiving or understanding. Yet Hegel immediately shifts over to the next concept and starts the whole process again. Where can one find the third level? It is perhaps not too much to suggest that it is found in the very act of displaying the movement of thought itself—the writing of the logic. In thinking itself, thought particularizes its distinctive moments: being, nothing, the unity of being and nothing, the moments of becoming, and the sublation of becoming.

At first this division seems arbitrary; it "can only be provisional."[21] It is justified when one understands the science and recognizes that the division must be integrated with the concept, or rather must lie within it. The divisions are the products of its own movement, of its self-determining, of its development. It involves a judgement, a primordial separation into opposites.

In other words, the division is the result of a process. It is a movement of self-determination.

But Hegel goes one step further, for the self-determining process has a presupposition—the integration of thinking and being in the *Phenomenology* which generated absolute knowing. It also has a posited result—the philosophy of the real: of nature and the social world of spirit.

The logic is defined as "the science of pure thought, the principle of which is *pure knowing*, the unity of which is not abstract but a living concrete unity."[22] Speculative reason understands that it is spirit that is self-determining, the spirit that comes to know itself in the *Phenomenology* and that comes to know the world in the philosophy of the real. This knowledge is what ensures that the self-determination of pure intelligence is not simply a pattern of pure thinking, but a metaphysics—the principles that govern all reality.

So we return to our starting point. The movement of intelligence is not simply the movement within an individual mind or an individual culture. It is the movement that characterizes the natural as well as the social order. The *Logic* contains the inherent principles that govern the universe, and have found their explicit self-determining expression in pure thought, whether practised by an individual, by a school, or by the full accumulation of intellectual traditions. Spirit is the unity that reflects on itself, and thus determines itself and divides itself.

It is through this act of comprehensive self-reference that the operations of understanding, dialectic, and speculative reason recur within the framework of understanding itself.

This proposal, however, takes us too far afield. It is sufficient to notice that the three operations function in an intricate and recursive way within the first chapter of the *Logic,* and that some of the plastic discourse displayed there may benefit from a plastic reception on the part of the reader.

III

Transition or Reflection

The term 'dialectic' seldom appears within the text of Hegel's *Science of Logic*. That work relies on "transition" or "becoming," "reflection," and "conceiving," all terms that take their place within the systematic progression from indeterminate being to self-determining method.[1] Yet in the second edition of "The Doctrine of Being," Hegel adds a passage that refers explicitly to dialectical development:

> In the various circles of determining, and particularly in the progress of the exposition (or rather in the progress of the concept to its exposition) a primary task is always to distinguish clearly between what is simply *in itself* and what is *posited:* between how the determinations are when in the concept, and how they are when posited or when there for another. This is a distinction which belongs only to the dialectical development, and which the metaphysical way of philosophizing (and that includes the critical) knows not.[2]

What distinguishes a dialectical development is the distinction between what is inherent and what is posited.

There is evidence to suggest that Hegel saw the importance of this distinction only after completing the first edition of Book I. In the edition of 1812, Hegel's move from "A Being in general" to "Something" goes by way of "Otherness," "Being-for-another and Being-in-itself," and "Reality." When summarizing this movement in the early paragraphs of "Something," he notes that 'a being' is the immediate union of 'being' and 'nothing', but 'reality' has introduced the difference between 'being-in-itself' and 'being-for-another' as determinations of reflection:

19

Reality is this unity in the determinate distinction of its moments, which constitute with respect to it diverse *sides* or determinations of reflection that are indifferent to each other.[3]

By the second edition, Hegel has transferred the discussion of 'being-in-itself' and 'being-for-another' to a stage subsequent to 'something'.[4] And in his remarks on this development he denies to these two "sides" of 'something' the status of determinations of reflection. The passage is sufficiently important to be quoted at length:

Being-in-itself at first has being-for-another as its opposite moment; but being-posited has also been opposed to it. In this latter expression being-for-another is, to be sure, included; but it explicitly contains that which is not in-itself as already folded back into whatever is its being-in-itself (whereby it is *positive*). *Being-in-itself* is usually to be taken as an abstract way of expressing the concept; *positing* occurs first only in the sphere of Essence, of objective reflection.... In the sphere of Being 'a being' only *proceeds* from 'becoming'; or with 'something' 'another' is posited, with 'finite', 'infinite'.[5] However 'finite' has not elicited the 'infinite'; it has in no way *posited* it. In the sphere of Being the *self-determining* of the concept is only *in itself*, and so it is called a transition. In a similar way the reflective determinations of Being (such as 'something' and 'other', or 'finite' and 'infinite'), even though they are essentially directed towards each other (or are to be beings-for-another), have a qualitative status, persisting on their own account: *the other is*; the finite functions as an immediate being and as fixed on its own account to the same extent as the infinite does. The sense of each appears to be complete without its counterpart. On the other hand, 'positive' and 'negative', or 'cause' and 'effect', for all that they are also to be taken as isolated, have at the same time no sense apart from each other.[6]

Here, although with 'something' 'another' is posited, they do not posit each other. Rather than being determinations of reflection (as they are in the first edition) each subsists qualitatively on its own account.

This significant refinement in the second edition immediately precedes the reference to dialectic cited earlier. It thus provides us with some evidence for our investigation concerning the nature of dialectic: What is it that distinguishes one logical moment as *in itself* or inherent, and another as posited reflectively?[7]

I

In the first edition, Hegel initiates "A being as such" with the phrase: "A being as such determines itself with respect to itself."[8] The reflexive but active verb is deleted from the second edition. In its place is added the sentence: "From becoming proceeds a being."[9] The long passage cited above draws attention to that distinction: "In the sphere of Being 'a being' only *proceeds* from 'becoming'." And again, "In the sphere of Being the *self-determining* of the concept is only *in itself*, and so it is called a transition."[10] The active force of "determines itself" is reserved to the concept. As immediate or in itself, this dynamic simply happens. One uses the phrases "proceeds out of," "passes over," or "transition."

'Transition' or 'passing over' first appears in the *Logic* in the section "Becoming." After the thought of being turns out to be of nothing, and the thought of nothing turns out to be of being, Hegel writes: "What is true is neither being nor nothing; but rather that being does not *pass over* into nothing, nor that nothing *passes over* into being, but that they *have passed over*."[11] Yet the two terms are not identical; they are to be distinguished absolutely. The immediate happening that has been discovered after the fact is not simply a collapse into an undifferentiated whole, but has involved a movement, a becoming. Hegel uses the perfect tense of "pass over" not because it is something that is not there at all, but because the transition is evident only in its result. The immediacy of the transition hides it from reflective thought at the moment of its happening. In thinking one thought, we have simply found ourselves thinking another without any sense of how that had occurred. After the fact, thought becomes aware that a transition has taken place. Once thought has identified this transition it can be given the name "becoming." This new term thus becomes the basis for further development.

This early passage suggests that the categories or terms that appear in Hegel's *Logic* do not simply represent ontological reality as that which comprehends all things visible and invisible, but rather signify transitions of thought. For in describing the transitions from 'being' to 'nothing' and vice versa, Hegel appeals not to some independent reality sensed or intuited, but to the operations of intuiting and of thinking. The transition has occurred within those operations that he later characterized in his psychology of intelligence.[12] Since each subsequent intellectual transition will pass from something determinate to something else, the name for that transition (or becoming) will reflect that greater determination. In this way, since a transition can be recognized only after it has happened, different conceptual categories will appear as the logic proceeds.

The changes introduced into the second chapter suggest that Hegel recognized that this program had not been consistently followed in the *Logic*'s first edition. There 'nothing' *had been posited* in 'a being', and it was this *reflective* determination that required the complementary thought of 'a non-being' or 'otherness'. The difference that 'reality' introduces is not the result of a simple transition, but has been *posited* by *reflection* when it added to the immediate content of 'a being' its remembered parentage. The move came from outside the immediate concept.

In the second edition, the logical development is more subtle. 'A being' is an immediate concept whose mediating 'becoming' has disappeared from view. To define it, thought simply places it beside the only other immediate concept it yet has: 'being.' 'Being' was completely indeterminate; 'a being' is something qualified. 'Quality' does not presuppose the contrast between 'a being' and 'a non-being' as 'otherness' had done. It is rather the result of a first hesitant transition from the immediacy of 'a being.' Similarly 'another' now names the result of a different immediate transition that occurs when 'something' is thought; the transition itself is named 'altering'.[13] The *Logic* then goes on to 'otherness', 'being-in-itself', and 'being-for-another'.[14]

II

Because Hegel discriminates between the immediate transitions that occur in the logic of being and more reflective considerations, his logic cannot leave the science of pure thought at the level of simply thinking thoughts and then passing over to other thoughts. A stream of consciousness is quite different from a systematic development. Indeed the category "becoming" is identified because subsequent thought has noticed its having passed over from one term to its contrary. Holding the first thought together with the second so that their opposition and the transition from one to the other is noticed is not a function of what is immediate. It involves reflection on what has happened—a process of determining what is essential. As Henrich has recognized, the description of the logic of being requires the use of operations that are fully characterized only in the logic of essence.[15]

Reflection, writes Hegel, is "the movement of becoming and passing over that remains within itself."[16] Rather than simply passing over from one thought to another, it persists through the transition, so that the difference is only a show, and what is essential is what is common.

In the immediacy of being, as we have seen, the transition is not something recognized in its occurrence, but only after it has hap-

pened. Therefore the commonness that reflection posits is not immediately evident but is retrospectively introduced by bringing the starting point and the result together into a synthesis. This act of synthesis
cancels the transition in which something has passed over to something else. But since that which differentiates the starting point from
the result is contrary to the commonness implicit in the synthesis,
each of the terms in its distinctness is also considered negatively.

Reflection, then, never simply accepts what is presented to it. It
takes both its terms and the transitions of thought differently from the
way they show themselves. This negative approach to its content con-
ceals the positivity implicit in the act of synthesis. Reflection uses an
immediate synthetic act to evaluate critically what is shown to it, and
to determine the essence that is not immediately present.

This double character of reflection as both explicitly negative and
implicitly positive contrasts with transition which, as immediate, is
explicitly positive but, as passing over to something else, is implicitly
negative. Through this contrast it can be characterized more precisely.

Hegel does so through three stages of his analysis. In the first
place, reflection presupposes that there is something positive—an
essence—that underlies the differences, and therefore it posits a relation between the two terms. The relation is placed in the terms by
reflection—is posited—in such a way that each term in turn posits, or
requires, its contrary.[17] Thus the categories of reflection are not taken
simply each on its own account, but each embodies a reference to its
counterpart.

In the second place, the fact that reflection posits and presupposes something positive and does so with respect to that which, though
immediate, had been taken in a negative way has a self-reflexive
implication. For reflection recognizes that its own operation is inherent neither in the immediate transition nor in the presupposed relation. It is rather external to both. In other words the negativity that is
explicit in the immediate content of reflection rebounds to characterize reflection itself.

In the third place, there is a significant consequence for reflection:
as external to that upon which it reflects it is not inherently determined by it. Therefore what it posits and presupposes may not be
what is in fact essential. In other words, its act of synthesis does not
inevitably make explicit the inherent positive relation that persists
through the transition. Reflection requires in addition principles that
on the one hand will justify its conclusions concerning what is essential, and that on the other are functions of its own reflective dynamic.
These principles will determine both the way reflection operates and
the positive content of reflection's object.

Hegel develops these determinations of reflection—which at the same time are the essentials of its own operations—through the second chapter of "The Doctrine of Essence." Identity, difference, diversity, opposition, and contradiction lead to the ultimate determining principle, or ground—that which provides a sufficient reason for its conclusions.

Under this interpretation, Hegel's three sections on positing reflection, external reflection, and determining reflection do not describe three species of reflection, each of which operates according to distinct principles. Three features of any reflection, they have become progressively identified as reflection has become more thoroughly self-reflexive. The full operation of reflection synthesizes what appears immediately as diverse, thereby positing and presupposing a common essence: in itself it is external to its subject-matter, but it uses as its principles of determination the fundamental laws of thought.[18]

This characterization of reflection has a significant implication for our project: if reflection is external to its subject matter, then a crucial distinction is introduced between the two. For that subject matter is simply presented as diverse and different. Any inherent transition has disappeared from view, creating ambiguity. When reflection synthesizes different thoughts, is it bringing together things that already have some inherent relation, or is it arbitrarily integrating a diverse multitude? The subsequent use of the determinations of reflection does not suffice to differentiate what is genuinely essential from what is accidental and contingent. For any thorough use of the determinations of reflection, Hegel argues, will inevitably lead to an explicit contradiction. And while a contradiction may be used as evidence of the falseness of one's premises, it may also be a stage on the way to discovering the grounds of the contradiction—to discovering the essence that underlies the initial relation. Which option one chooses will depend on whether one is convinced that there is an inherent relation to be explicated or not; that conviction begs the question that is to be decided through the contradiction.

Reflection, then, in that it is external to its subject matter, is intrinsically conditioned by contingency.[19] Self-reflexivity can become aware of that contingency, but it is impotent to overcome it. Since it remains external to its subject matter even in being self-reflexive, it can never ensure that its reflection is a direct function of that subject matter either in its original synthesis or in its determining operation.

III

We have distinguished the inherent transitions of becoming from the posited externality of reflection as was required by dialectical development.[20] But instead of achieving systematic integrity, the two have fallen apart into diverse operations of thought. Transitions are immediate and inherent, but are noticed only after they have occurred. Because reflection is subsequent and synthetic, it is necessarily external to the relations it considers. If this were all, Hegel would be left with the perpetually incomplete dialectic of Sartre, in which the *pour soi* (or reflection) can never catch up with the *en soi* (or immediacy).[21]

But this is not all; for both the immediate transition and the external reflection are operations of thought. As such they are moments within a comprehensive context. If the nature of that context can be carefully individuated and thus distinguished from its two operations, then we will have established not only the inherent integrity of dialectical development but also the systematic nature of the *Science of Logic*.

Earlier we identified the subject of the transitions of becoming as the intelligence of Hegel's psychology. Intelligence is also the agent of reflection. What the *Logic* requires to be complete, then, is a discussion of intelligence as the comprehensive context of both transition and reflection—the context that determines the one to be immediate and the other to be external to that immediacy. To this context, Hegel gives the name "concept."[22]

Henrich bypasses the logic of concept in his discussion of method because the two concepts of 'universality' and 'particularity' are only contraries and do not incorporate the full weight of contradiction.[23] But the act of conceiving does not involve simply generalizing and specifying—the acts named by those two categories. Conceiving is the comprehensive operation of intelligence that determines itself by specifying its own moments. The negative moment of specifying can itself be specified. As contrary to generality, it is not itself a concept. Since it cannot be thought, it can only be indicated. By applying the particularizing act self-referentially, thought no longer thinks, but only refers. And it refers to a singular individual. "Determinacy that relates itself to itself is individuality."[24] The moment of pure reference entails as its counterpart the self-referential discrimination of its contradictory—generalizing thought which now lacks concrete reference. Universality becomes something purely abstract, lacking the concreteness of immediate individuality. The contradictories in "The Doctrine of Conceiving," then, are abstract universality and individuality.

Conceiving is not a synthetic operation bringing together an externally related transition and reflection—it does not reproduce at a higher level the activity of reflective thought. Quite the contrary. It considers itself, the comprehensive totality of intelligence already present. And it specifies within itself two contradictory moments: the pure immediacy of its dynamic that, as individual, can only be refer-

entially indicated; and its generalizing synthesis or abstract universality. It disjoins transition and reflection[25] by self-referentially individuating its own disjunctive operation. Through applying disjunctive
inference to itself, it isolates the immediate transitions of the logic of
being, positing them as moments of its own determinate content; and
it identifies the external syntheses of reflection with the abstract universality that is the other moment of the disjunction. The two contradictories are in fact products of a single act which does not create
itself thereby, but only renders itself more determinate.[26]

Within this general context, conceiving is another name for understanding.[27] When it is not used self-referentially to discriminate its own
operations, it may result in the fixity of dead thought. When applied
consistently and thoroughly, even to itself, understanding articulates
the self-determining nature of comprehensive intelligence.[28]

Conceptual thought disjoins its immediate transitions and its
reflective syntheses—its individuality and its abstract universality.
This initial act grounds the logical development, for reflection and the
immediacy it reflects upon are the two contradictory sides of a single
conceptual totality. When intelligence explicitly knows itself as the
subject of the *Logic*, the logical development ceases to be arbitrary and
relative, but becomes necessary and absolute.

IV

Hegel's reference to dialectic in the second edition of the *Logic* uses
this tripartite schema. Dialectical development is contrasted to metaphysical and critical philosophy because it differentiates what is
inherent from what is posited, "how the determinations are when in
the concept, and how they are when posited or when there for another."[29] In positing this distinction between immediate transitions and
reflective positings, dialectic also disjoins them as contradictory
moments within its own dynamic.

In the *Logic* all three moments—transition, reflection and disjunction—are operations of intelligence or pure thought. If this is the only
description of dialectic, Marx's response is justified: Hegel needs to be
put back on his feet. For the realm of pure thought appears to have
nothing to do with the material reality that is other than, and therefore outside of, thought's comprehension.[30]

For Marx the immediate transitions are not intellectual but material. What simply happens is a temporal, material process, intuited
directly by the senses. Reflection is the response of thought to that
matter, and is therefore derivative. As external it is bedevilled by con-

tingency; it does not determine what is genuinely essential, but produces rather an ideology. It reflects what only appears essential to a finite consciousness.

Praxis takes over from understanding the function of disjunctive integration.[31] In a single act it disjoins the immediacy of historical action and the reflective syntheses of abstract thought. Consciously revolutionary, it is aware of both starting point and result while immersed in an immediate transition of history. It is dialectical because it maintains the radical disjunction that combines 'both/and' and 'either/or'.

No less than Marx, however, Hegel recognizes the bare externality and radical contingency of the world of nature and of history. In the philosophies of nature and of spirit he shows how external natural transitions in their contingency may be reflectively appropriated by thought to determine their relative necessity. But for a science to reach true conclusions more is required. The disjunction of immediacy and reflection needs to be the product of a self-determining agent; the immediacy of nature in its contingent externality must be individuated not simply in a finite moment of praxis, but comprehensively in all time and space. For the intelligent agent needs to know that his disjunctive operations reproduce the comprehensive agency that on the one hand grounds nature's temporal processes and that on the other generates synthetic unities in nature and history.

This is why Hegel requires the Christian doctrines of creation and reconciliation. The former posits the transitions of nature, the latter identifies the finite individuals with its own dynamic. Without the clear disjunction of these two cosmic operations, Hegel's system ceases to be absolute, and dialectic is no longer "the only true method"[32] but only one ideology among many.

IV

Where is the Place of Understanding?

Understanding has had a bad press amongst Hegelians. "However much Understanding may be the foundation of the sciences and of practical life, and must serve as a beginning to philosophy," writes John Findlay, "it will none the less lead to thwarted and arrested development if it is allowed to dominate philosophical thinking."[1]

Errol Harris comments: "The understanding restricts itself to the finite, and its thinking is always finite thinking.... That is why its objects are always abstract and separated from the matrix in which they are, in truth, actually embedded as moments of an infinite process through which an infinite whole develops itself."[2]

A third example comes from Merold Westphal: "The task, which Understanding finds impossible, is so to remain in control of oneself in giving oneself up to the mediating activity of the other that the whole operation can be called a self-mediating activity."[3]

Findlay and Harris admit that there is a role for understanding to play. Faced with paragraphs 79 to 82 of the *Encyclopaedia*, they allow that the understanding has a subordinate function in intellectual discourse and action. Hegel, after all, when lecturing on the paragraph on understanding[4] comments that "Understanding is as indispensable in practice as it is in theory." But its fixity and accuracy are soon to be overwhelmed by the effects of dialectical and speculative reason.

It is not simply in the introduction to the *Encyclopaedia*, however, where understanding is discussed positively. There is also a bit of praise in the preface to the *Phenomenology*. "Analysis," writes Hegel, "only arrives at *thoughts* which are themselves familiar, fixed, and inert determinations. But what is thus *separated* and non-actual is an essential moment; for it is only because the concrete does divide itself, and makes itself into something non-actual, that it is self-moving. The activity of dissolution is the power and work of the *Understanding*, the most astonishing and mightiest of powers, or rather the absolute power."[5]

From this passage one draws the conclusion that Hegel's judgement on understanding is at least ambivalent. It is not an operation that is simply forgotten once we enjoy the vision of the whole or the sense of the compatibility of opposites. It is, in fact, the motive power of philosophical thinking—it generates a process of destruction that dissolves wholes into parts. And it is only because Spirit neither shrinks from death nor keeps itself untouched by devastation, but instead endures death and maintains itself therein,[6] that genuine philosophical wisdom becomes possible.

This strong claim about the essential role of understanding in philosophy, expressed so eloquently in the preface to the *Phenomenology*, is reproduced, as we have seen, in the small section of the *Encyclopaedia* that introduces the logic as such: the section entitled "Logic further defined and divided."[7] This was not an addition to the 1827 edition, although its location immediately preceding "The Doctrine of Being" is new. In 1817, Hegel placed the four paragraphs on the three "sides" of the logic at the very beginning of "Preliminary Notion"— right after the antecedent of what later became paragraph 19.

Between 1807 and 1817 Hegel had produced the *Science of Logic*. We might well presume that the passage introduced into the *Encyclopaedia* was designed to summarize the "method" of that logical system. We are, then, faced with a question: Where in the larger *Logic* does Hegel discuss the role of understanding?

From the order of the *Encyclopaedia*'s list: understanding, dialectical reason, and speculative reason, we might well presume that understanding has its place at the beginning of the logic. But it does not take very long before we become uncomfortable with that conclusion. The first concept, 'being,' is almost the exact opposite of understanding. It is indeterminate, lacking any distinctions and divisions, whereas understanding involves "fixity of determinations and their distinctness from one another."[8] The concept 'being' cannot be the expression of understanding as such.

Perhaps, then, it is not in the concept, but what happens to the concept. In thinking pure being, thought finds itself thinking nothing. By reflecting on that transition it identifies the most primitive feature of thought, which it calls 'becoming'. 'Becoming' names the process in which the thought of 'being' passes over into its opposite, 'nothing'. But this process is described in the *Encyclopaedia* passage under a different paragraph. It is not through understanding but "in the dialectical stage [where] finite characterizations or formulae supersede themselves and pass into their opposites."[9]

Becoming, and its more developed forms of alteration, repulsion and attraction, continuity and relation do not develop the explanation and description of understanding, but rather the various characteristics of dialectical reason.

If understanding is not described in the beginning, is it picked up in the intermediate discussion of essence? After all, the power of the negative that Hegel describes in the *Phenomenology* is not a starting point, but a mediation that breaks up the circle from which it began on the way towards a more comprehensive perspective.

Here again our quest is unsuccessful. For, in the early stages of essence, thought shifts back and forth from essential to inessential, from show to essence. What happens here is not simply the immediate transitions or passings over that characterize being. Rather, the process of becoming is now taken together with its starting point and its result, so that the whole complex becomes the focus of attention. We became aware of 'becoming' only because we found ourselves at a different place from where we thought we were. In thinking 'essence', we are aware of a larger picture because the focus is constantly shifting, as in a holograph. This perpetual flickering from one notion to its contrary and back again is now being considered as a whole. To this sense of the whole Hegel gives the name "reflection." Reflection first synthesizes the complex, recognizes that it itself stands outside of the complex, and then establishes the determinate structures that define the essence both of the complex and of its recognition. In other words, reflection considers the reciprocal flickering as a unity which has permanent determinations that help to constitute the opposition between two sides. It comprehends both dissolution and transition.

The process of positing and determining sounds as if it might reflect the act of understanding. But once again we are deceived. For my description of reflection is captured by Hegel, not in the paragraph on understanding, but in the paragraph on speculative reason: "The Speculative stage, or stage of Positive Reason, apprehends the unity of the determinations in their opposition,—the affirmative, which is involved in their disintegration and in their transition."[10]

This sense of unity in opposition is not only a feature of reflection, but is picked up throughout the doctrine of essence: as contradiction and ground; as the essential relations of whole and part, force and expression, outer and inner; and as the absolute relations of substance, cause, and reciprocity.

We are, then, left with only one option. The theory of understanding is developed in the doctrine of the concept. But this flies against all conventional wisdom. Errol Harris, for example, says that Hegel protests against the abstraction of traditional logic that says that "the concept is that of understanding, the abstract universal."[11] And Findlay introduces his discussion of concept or notion by referring to the way in which "the melting of the walls between interacting substances can, if it occurs at all, only be a *conscious melting....* The Notion is accordingly one with a man's thinking being, the same universal thinking nature in all...."[12] The melting of walls, even though it be conscious, cannot be correlated with "fixity of determinations and their distinctness from one another."

Nonetheless we should pause. Many commentators have wondered why Hegel, when he arrives at the freedom of the concept, proceeds to talk about the abstractions of formal logic, with its syllogisms and inferences. These seem to be the products of understanding; they are not simply criticized but, as always in Hegel's philosophy, given a positive and significant position within the total picture. Once the limitations of any thought, concept, or term is recognized it is left free to function without challenge.

The phrase "freedom of the concept" is itself intriguing. For it suggests the sphere of practice, and it reminds us that Hegel said in his lectures: "A man of character is an understanding man, who in that capacity has definite ends in view and undeviatingly pursues them." And "Understanding corresponds to what we call the goodness of God.... Under this shape Understanding is visible in every department of the objective world; and no object in that world can ever be wholly perfect which does not give full satisfaction to the canons of understanding."[13]

When we turn to examine the text of the larger *Logic* more closely, we find some surprising claims. Within the section on the particular concept, Hegel writes: "This is the impotence of nature, that it cannot adhere to and exhibit the strictness of the concept, and runs wild in this blind unconceptual multiplicity."[14] This claim that it is not the melting of the walls, but the strictness of fixed forms that defines the concept runs directly counter to Findlay's claim. And so it is perhaps not surprising that Johnston and Struthers, formed in an earlier Hegelianism, turned this sentence completely around: "This is the impotence of Nature, to hold fast and to represent the austerity of the Notion, so that it wastes away into this notionless and blind multiplicity."[15]

On looking further, we find precisely in the section on the particular concept an extended discussion of understanding.

Particularizing a concept involves abstracting a determination. The faculty of such abstraction is called understanding.[16] Such a process involves fixity and unalterability. But, says Hegel, "we must recognize the infinite force of the understanding in splitting the concrete into abstract determinations and plumbing the depth of the difference, the force that at the same time is alone the power that effects their transition."[17]

Far from adopting the light estimation and inferior ranking which had been applied to understanding by his contemporaries, Hegel here identifies it with the process of particularizing or determining a concept. And he attributes the fault of bare analysis not to understanding but to reason: "Since, therefore, understanding exhibits the infinite force which determines the universal, or conversely, imparts through the form of universality a fixity and subsistence to the determinateness that is in and for itself transitory, then it *is not the fault of the understanding* if no progress is made beyond this point. It is a subjective *impotence of reason* which adopts these determinatenesses in their fixity, and which is unable to bring them back to their unity through the dialectical force opposed to their abstract universality, in other words through their own peculiar nature, or through their Notion."[18]

The end of that citation suggests that the notion or concept is the remedy brought in to rectify the half-truth of understanding. But that suggestion is misleading, for the phrase "through their notion" is parallel to "through their own peculiar nature." How can we know the *peculiar* (*eigentümliche*) nature of the determinatenesses if we do not particularize that nature by means of the understanding? The suggestion here is that the way out of the fixity of understanding is not to be found by bringing in an antidote, but by following it through consistently to its limits.

Hegel goes on to make this explicit: "The highest maturity, the highest stage, which anything can attain is that in which its downfall begins. The fixity of the determinateness into which the understanding seems to run, the form of the imperishable, is that of self-relating universality. But this belongs properly to the Notion...." As a result, "the determinate and abstract Notion is the *condition*, or rather *an essential moment of reason....* Therefore the usual practice of separating understanding and reason is, from every point of view, to be rejected."[19]

There is an amazing suggestion here, if one has been reared on the traditional interpretation. The <u>highest</u> <u>achievement</u> of thought is <u>understanding</u>, <u>which</u> <u>actually</u> <u>brings</u> <u>about</u> the <u>destruction</u> of what has been achieved. This, indeed, is what then occurs in the *Logic*. For the next step is the process of particularizing the process of conceiving itself. By isolating and fixing the process of conceptual thought (or notion as the older school has it) one distinguishes it from that which cannot be conceived, or the simple singular.[20]

In the section on the particular concept, then, we find what we have been looking for: an explicit discussion of the role of understanding. And although it begins from the contemporary dismissal of understanding as contrary to reason, it ends by making understanding a condition and essential moment of reason. The process of particularizing and fixing determinations continues throughout the third book of the *Logic:* in the analysis of formal logic; in the discussion of systematic analyses, whether mechanical, chemical, or teleological; and in the discussion of the process by which subjective thought is applied to its objectivity in life, cognition, and finally pure method. What is happening here is a process of particularizing and singularizing, of identifying not only the constituent terms but also the relations between the terms. It is that process of full articulation—of bringing all the features to consciousness—which ends by admitting that thought is itself finite, and needs to surrender to externality. This admission opens up the possibility of a transition from logic to its antithesis, nature.[21]

In other words we are driven to take seriously the opening sentence of the chapter on the concept: "*Understanding* is the term usually employed to express the faculty of conceiving."[22]

Let us stop for a moment and consider where we are. Although in the *Encyclopaedia* Hegel outlines the three sides of logic in the order of understanding, dialectic and speculative reason, in the *Logic* he places understanding at the end, and calls it the highest maturity which anything can attain.

There is a phrase in paragraph 79 that should perhaps have been taken more seriously: "Logical doctrine has three sides." The word "sides" suggests a plane figure, and three sides refers to a triangle. Perhaps we have been wrong all along in looking for a first among the three. Perhaps, like a triangle on a plane, it can rotate, so that at various moments different sides are at the bottom, and different sides are at the top. The dissolution of understanding initiates the dialectic. The transitions of dialectic trigger the reflections of speculative reason, and the wholes of speculation are fixed and determined by understanding. The triangle becomes a rather lumping wheel, bumping its way through thought, nature, and the world of man.

I now draw three implications from my conclusion. First, if conceiving involves particularizing and not generalizing, then it is better to translate the German *Begriff* as "concept" than as "notion." In the preceding text I have cited Findlay and Miller, using their terminology. I trust it is understood that when I sometimes used "notion" and at other times used "concept" I was talking about the same thing. My Oxford English Dictionary defines "notion" with the term "concept," and notes that it is regularly used with "under": "Under the notion of...." This suggests that particulars would not be the ways the notion determines itself, but are rather items to be subsumed into the general. Concept, however, retains the sense of determinacy and particularizing, especially when it is expressed not by the simple noun, but by the gerund "conceiving." There is quite a difference between "the labor of the notion" (or alternatively "the labor of the concept") and "the labor of conceiving." If the concept involves moving from the universal to the particular using a process commonly called understanding, then the gerund is a useful way of glossing Hegel's text.

Once we do this, however, we are confronted with our second implication. Neither the right-wing nor the left-wing interpretation of Hegel is correct. For the left-wing Hegelians have made dialectic the foundation, and the right-wing Hegelians have made speculation ultimate. But if anything is right, it is that understanding clearly determines and fixes each of these moments within a triangle that includes all three. It alone is fully self-reflexive. In this way it establishes the *triangle* as ultimate, and not any one of its sides or points.

The right-wing interpretation takes Hegel's dictum: "The true is the whole" as normative. Therefore only when all determinations are speculatively reconciled in a comprehensive totality is some level of philosophical wisdom achieved. This interpretation rides uncomfortably with history, particularly the history after Hegel. Either you claim, with Kojève and Stanley Rosen that history stopped once Hegel published his *Phenomenology,* or you take the position of Findlay and others that the ultimate achievement of knowledge is to emerge from the cave and contemplate nontemporal truths.

The left-wing interpretation sees no final reconciliation but only a dialectical process, one that is always dissolving what is present and passing beyond it. History is taken seriously, because it is radically open. There will always be a movement to the opposite of what we now have; one can either become frustrated by trying to stop it, or get on the bandwagon and promote it.

But if we take seriously Hegel's statement that "the highest maturity, the highest stage which anything can attain is that in which its downfall begins," then we have to rethink our understanding of what is absolute and what is true in Hegel. For the implication of placing understanding's ability to fix and determine at the culmination of the logic, where logical theory is conscious of its own operations, is that there will be immediate dialectical transitions into opposites, and there will also be speculative reconciliations into wholes. But those reconciliations, once achieved, will be conceived, or understood. The constituent moments and the relations between them will become fully articulate. And that achievement will inevitably trigger another dialectical transition. Therefore *any* claim to absoluteness, *any* claim to truth, will discover that the very effort to fix the claim conceptually will result in its dissolution and downfall. This development must apply to Hegel's theory itself.

That being so, why does Hegel conclude his works with chapters called "Absolute Knowledge," "Absolute Idea," and "Absolute Spirit"? The answer to that question can only be provided by a detailed understanding of what is in fact described in those chapters.[23] But I will answer briefly by referring to an interesting statement in the introduction to the *Science of Logic:* "I could not pretend that the method which I follow in this system of logic—or rather which this system in its own self follows—is not capable of greater completeness, of much elaboration in detail; but at the same time I know that it is the only true method."[24]

Since the method is the lumpy, bumpy triangular wheel, it will involve both dialectic and speculation. Transitions are essential, and comprehensive wholes are essential. But this can be acknowledged only because understanding isolates and fixes each of them, and holds them together in a disjunction: either becoming or reflection. Both transition and reflection are essential constituents. And that disjunctive judgement is the culminating stage of the effort to couple the contradictory terms of conceptual thought—universal and singular—in a single perspective.[25]

In other words, dialectical transitions will introduce contingencies; reflection will integrate this new subject matter into a comprehensive perspective; understanding will fix its terms and relations. Each such move will involve elaboration in detail, and will move toward greater completeness, particularly as the results of all three are adequately understood. Such a development towards an open future is described in the culminating chapters of each of Hegel's three works: *Phenomenology, Logic,* and *Encyclopaedia.* The only thing which does not become relativized is the method itself. The inherent dynamic of proper knowing, of proper thinking, and of proper self-conscious life will embody its pattern and sequence. But, as we noted with respect to the chapter "Absolute Idea," where Hegel explicitly conceives the method, the achievement of understanding or conceiving results in the method acknowledging its own particularity; and its claim to be a complete perspective discovers its own partiality.[26]

In other words, by recognizing that speculative reason, dialectic, and understanding each has its place at the pinnacle of the method, we recognize that no immediate transition, no comprehensive vision, and no philosophical wisdom will ever be the last word. The only true method will see to it that another word will emerge. And that will happen because the understanding of the concept self-referentially understands that development as well as how the three sides of the one true method are related. This moment of self-reference it alone commands with full authority. And it produces the recognition that none of the three, including itself, is final.

My third and final comment concerns a more complex question. It is the thesis of Walter Zimmerli, among others, that what Hegel actually does in the *Logic* is not adequately described and explained in the theory of the concept.[27] There are inferences and arguments that are not captured in the formalism of judgement and syllogism.

The picture I have proposed suggests that Zimmerli has been looking for the wrong thing, and in the wrong place. Careful analysis of a number of logical transitions has shown that, inevitably, they start with the effort to isolate, conceive, or understand a concept; that this leads to a transition in which the original concept dissolves into its opposite; that this result is reflectively taken together with its starting point; and that this synthesis, carefully understood, unfolds a network of terms and relations that are integrated into a unity. In other words, understanding has generated a new concept.

I trust it is clear from what I have already said that these stages of the logical operation are in fact described in the various books of the *Logic:* dialectical transition is explored in the doctrine of being; reflective synthesis and integration in the doctrine of essence; understanding's precision in the doctrine of conceiving. On one level, then, the logic as a whole self-reflectively describes the structure of its constituent transitions.

But what, then, is happening in the doctrine of the concept? Here, instead of describing a process, we are trying to conceive it: to determine its particular constituents. This will involve identifying the terms and the relations as independent determinations and thinking through the way they function within an integrated unity.

Hegel is claiming in the first part of the doctrine of the concept that the structures of formal logic are not simply arbitrary. When they are set in context—that is, when each one is both understood in its own terms and taken together with the dialectical transitions that result from that understanding—they define the constituent stages of logical reasoning.

The process of conceiving, or particularizing, passes over from a universal concept to a singular. This is a simple becoming, a move of dialectical reason. Judgement speculatively holds opposites together, starting from singular and abstract universal in the positive judgement, and culminating with both/and and either/or in the disjunctive judgement. The discussion of the modal judgements introduces the need to conceive necessity. Finally, the syllogism understands or conceives the necessity of the logic, and that culminates in the disjunctive syllogism. There the major premise is the speculative synthesis; the inference is a dialectical process of particularizing that universal into a singular. The act of conceiving—of understanding—is here fully understood.

These structures are the formal pattern of what in fact occurs within every logical and philosophical move. But they can only be appropriated if they are seen to be the efforts to *understand* the processes already described in the earlier parts of the *Logic:* to conceive what has emerged; to take what is present in its totality and define its determinations.

We have, then, found an answer for Job's question: Where is the place of understanding? Its destructive capacity ensures that it is not to be found in the land of the living; its abstract formalism means that man knoweth not the price thereof. But, as Job suggests, the place of understanding is where wisdom will be found (Job 28:12f).

V

The Necessity of Contingency

An analysis of Hegel's chapter, "Actuality":
Science of Logic, Book II, Part 3, Chapter 2

In an article published in 1958, Dieter Henrich wrote: "According to Hegel's theory, contingency itself is necessary without qualification."[1] Henrich's purpose in that paper did not require an examination in detail of Hegel's justification for this claim. Since, however, the strength of Hegel's philosophy lies not simply in its comprehensive scope, but also in the detailed execution of each link, this chapter will pick up Henrich's point that Hegel establishes the necessity of contingency, and will explore the way it is defended within the pages of the larger *Logic* by reconstructing the argument in the chapter, "Actuality."

Hegel calls his logic "the system of pure reason"[2] and "the science of the pure Idea, that is, the Idea in the abstract element of thought."[3] It proceeds, free from the specific content of sensible intuition and experience. Indeed, its intellectual activity probes beyond the representations and ideas which are but indirect generalizations from experience, either arbitrarily universal or concretely expressed in metaphor and illustration. The content of the logic is that which is present when pure thought simply thinks concepts and categories apart from their application and use. To become a science, and hence an ordered discipline, however, thought must also articulate the *relations* between concepts with precision and clarity.[4] It cannot, in its turn, proceed by means of arbitrary intuition or insightful analogy. For Hegel it employs the reflective procedures of thought: the careful understanding of determinate, positive characteristics; the dialectical

39

implications of that determination; and reflection which integrates these specific contrary terms into a speculative, inclusive unity.[5] These three logical procedures—understanding, dialectical and speculative reason—will provide the schematic structure of our analysis.

Contingency, or Formal Actuality, Possibility, and Necessity

As a first step in exploring the necessity of contingency, we must understand clearly what "contingency" means. "The contingent," writes Hegel, "is an actual which is determined at the same time only as possible—whose other, or opposite, is just as [possible]."[6] In this statement are included two words which are themselves highly ambiguous in ordinary usage: actual and possible. To understand precisely what is involved in contingency, then, these concepts must be clarified in turn.[7]

1. When thought first considers the concept 'actuality', it is taken to be synonymous with 'being', or with 'existence'. 'What is actual' seems to be similar to the expressions 'what is' and 'what exists'. But careful reflection leads to more precise discriminations. In the first place, 'what is' is more abstract than either of the other two expressions; in the second place, the existence of an entity is distinguished from its essence, whereas 'actual' incorporates the sense of actualizing the essence. That essence, capable of being actualized, is more precisely thought of as the possibility of the actual. That the actual actualizes the possible specifies its difference from the apparently synonymous terms: 'being' and 'existence'. Dialectic has led us to the term 'possibility' which we now need to explore if we are to complete our understanding of 'actuality'.[8]

2. The possible is the ground of the actual. As ground, however, it is not simply other than the actual, for it is implicitly what the actual is explicitly. This identity of the implicit and the explicit defines the positive sense of 'possibility', while its distinction from the actual provides its negative determination.[9]

There are, then, two distinct sides to the meaning of possibility. On the one hand it is intrinsically related to, but other than, the actual and not positively definable on its own. On the other hand, it has the positive sense of being the self-identity of the actual. For the actual is possible because it does not contradict itself. Compared to the simple and immediate sense of 'actuality' with which we began, this double sense of 'possibility' is complex and dialectical. Reflection must explore how the two distinct senses are related.[10]

We take the positive sense first. What is possible is self-identical. In other words, everything is possible which does not contradict itself. The universality of that statement, however, poses problems. For the term 'everything' includes within its range all distinct possibilities, some of which will contradict others. Therefore there is a sense in which every-thing—stressing the potential universality of every—is not possible.[11]

This dialectical paradox becomes explicit when thought does not think about possibility in general, but about a specific possible. If some-thing, let us say A, is possible, then according to the positive meaning of the term, A is self-identical, or A = A. But according to that same def-inition, the opposite or contrary of A is also possible, since what is not A is what is not A: -A = -A. While *each* of A and -A is thus possible, it is not possible for *both* to be possible, since A & -A is a contradiction, and not self-identical. At this point the second aspect of possibility appears, since it is not possible for both possibles to become actual.[12]

Speculative reason finds that it is faced with an intriguing dialec-tic. It began thinking of possibility as the ground of the actual—what the actual actualizes. In its positive sense, however, the possible is what is self-identical. Reflection on the latter has shown that it is no longer possible to claim that the actual is simply the possible actual-ized. For a distinction has been introduced between possibles which have been actualized, and those which thus cannot be. Thought must now understand the significance of this new sense of 'actuality' which incorporates all the distinctions that have so far emerged.[13]

3. The actual still is intrinsically possible. The immediate identity remains. But the possible per se is only possible and is not inevitably actualized. Therefore the actual, as now thought, is not simply the pos-sible, but only one possible of many. This complex reflection, which includes possibility as only possible, transcends and cancels the original sense of 'the actual'. Indeed, since that original immediate sense did not distinguish between possibles, it is now evident that it did not do justice to the more inclusive sense of 'actuality' now developed. As the simple identity of actuality and possibility, it was only a possibility itself.[14]

But this implies in turn that possibilities are actual. To be sure, they are not *really* actual, or absolutely and completely actual. The sense is rather that original one where actuality can barely be distin-guished from the vague generality of being, or the universality of simple existence. Possibilities are immediately present to thought. *In this sense*, all possibilities are, have existence, and are actual.[15]

On the other hand, the more developed sense of 'actual', as that which actualizes one of several possibilities, brings us to the defini-tion of contingent with which we began. For, you will recall, "the con-tingent is an actual which is determined at the same time only as possible—whose other, or opposite, is just as possible." From our review we can now see that by 'actual' we mean an existing actual which has actualized one possibility out of many. The other term 'possible' means simply that which is self-identical, and which can be thought without contradiction. That the one particular possibility becomes actual is not the inevitable result of its possibility, but is itself contingent.[16]

What are the implications of this definition of 'contingent'? In the first place, there is no reason or ground why the contingent actual, rather than its opposite, was actualized. Whatever ground it has is simply its own actuality. To this extent it is groundless. Similarly, the range of self-identical possibilities is indifferent to its multiplicity and implicit contradictions. There is nothing within any particular possible that can explain the actuals that do result. They, too, lack any inherent ground or justification. Therefore, within the meaning of contingency, both the actual and the possible are groundless.[17]

But this is not the total picture. For the 'actual' is defined as that which actualizes the possible. The two terms are used in the definition of contingency because the actual is, in some sense, grounded in the possible. Similarly, the possible is thought of as self-identical because it is implicitly what the actual is explicitly. Its meaning is grounded in the actual. Thus the term 'contingency' also includes within its meaning the mutual grounding of the actual in the possible and of the possible in the actual.[18]

In other words, analysis of the meaning of 'contingency' gives the paradoxical conclusion that, as contingent, it lacks a ground, and, as contingent, it is grounded.[19]

In thinking through this contradiction implicit in the term 'contingency', thought finds itself moving from moment to moment with a restless somersaulting of meanings. Four stages can be distinguished:[20]

1. The contingent *actual* is thought of as immediately one with its possibility—with what it is in itself. It is simple existence without a ground. Yet, lacking a ground which it actualizes it loses the distinctive sense of 'actual'. It is simply *possible*.
2. The *actual* is thought of as distinct from the possible which is its ground. But the possible is not sufficient to ground its actuality as contingent, since it is only one of a number of *possibles*.
3. The *possible* is thought in its simple, positive sense of self-identity. But as such it does have actuality in the universal sense of 'that which is'. It is immediately *actual*.
4. The *possible*, thought of as distinct from, and reflectively derived from, the actual lacks actuality. But even so it has a

bare existence which is not reflectively constituted. Again it is immediately *actual*.[21]

In the concept 'contingency', 'actual' and 'possible' are taken, first in their immediate positive senses, and then as distinct from their contraries. But none of these four senses remains where it began: it converts into its opposite. This total conversion of senses is the result when thought endeavors to render the concept 'contingency' determinate. Yet that concept incorporates all of these aspects. Understanding this complex identity leads to a strange implication. For an actuality that is the same as its possibility, and a possibility that is nothing other than actual, is necessary. When the process of transition from one meaning into another is collapsed into a simple unity, 'contingency' is no longer the appropriate term.[22]

This curious consequence needs to be justified. What is necessary is an actual that is both immediately present and needs no further justification. Since the actualization of one possibility excludes its opposite from being actualized, the latter is thereby rendered impossible. But that whose opposite is not possible is necessary. As actual, then, the necessary is immediate and not grounded in something else, yet it *is* grounded in its own intrinsic possibility, since its opposite is impossible. In this sense, 'the necessary' is an actual that is intrinsically its own possibility, and thus lacks a ground, while being yet grounded in that possibility. And its possibility is simply its own actuality, even though it is thought as possible through reflection on that actuality. The complex of meanings that resulted from a careful understanding of the meaning of 'contingency' turns out to be identical with this formal sense of 'necessity' as that whose opposite is not possible. In the meaning of 'contingency' the various moments are left distinct and are not thought together. In the meaning of 'necessity' they are explicitly integrated, and the distinctions are left implicit. In this sense, then, 'the contingent' is the same as 'the necessary'.[23]

We would seem to have reached the goal of our quest. For the meaning of 'contingency', when thoroughly explored, is shown to be identical with the meaning of 'necessity'. Therefore what is contingent is necessary. But the subject of that sentence ("what is contingent") refers to the meaning as relationship of moments; the predicate ("necessary") refers to the meaning as unity.

A moment's reflection will lead to dissatisfaction with that result. We have defined 'necessity' in a purely formal sense as the reflective impossibility of the opposite of any given actuality. It is the unity of possibility as ground and of actuality as groundless. But these two terms have been equally formal and independent of content. The actual is simply what is, and the possible is simply self-identity. These are not the only senses of those terms, and therefore the result is a somewhat specious victory. For the necessity of contingency as yet established would lead to no more than the concession that whatever is actual is necessary, since what is actual cannot be otherwise. Although this sense of 'necessity' was used in the argument for fatalism developed by the Megarans, it does not cover the sense of 'necessity' which is more common in the contemporary world. Hegel himself recognized this consequence. So he takes us further in exploring what the necessity of contingency could mean.

Relative Necessity, or Real Actuality, Possibility, and Necessity

1. In fact, we have already begun the further development of his argument. As we have seen, the formally necessary is a contingent actual. But it is not an actual as simple being, or bare existence. It is an actual determined to be *one* self-identical possible and which thereby *excludes* others. In contrast to the earlier, pre-reflective sense of 'actual', this includes those precise determinations which have resulted from reflection. As determinate, it is thought of as real. Understanding must now determine what this more developed sense of 'actual' is.[24]

The real actual is a thing with many determinate properties. But the term 'actual' is not simply equivalent to the thing as distinct from its properties, nor to existence as distinct from appearance. It has, in addition, the sense of *activity*—of actualizing through its own inherent dynamic what it is in itself.[25]

2. As we have seen in the previous section, that which is actualized is the possible. When, however, we look for that which makes possible real actuals, we are not satisfied with the formal definition of self-identity. Instead, the possibility of an actual is the dynamic ground, "pregnant with content," out of which the specific characteristics are actualized. In other words, it is a 'real possibility' in both senses of the phrase: it is a real *possibility* as that which has the likelihood of becoming actual; it is *real* possibility as the full range of actual conditions which are sufficient to generate that which they condition. Reflective thought once again becomes speculative as it explores the tension between these two senses that have dialectically emerged from 'real actuality'.[26]

Real possibilities are *actual* conditions. Each one is an actuality as well as a possibility. But the identity is an identity of content—of the particular determination that is thus characterized. After all, it is not the possibility of its own actuality. It is a possible only through its rela-

tion, as ground, to *another* actuality. Reflection has exposed this relation to the actuality towards which it is directed. On the other hand, for
reflection to determine the real possibility of some actuality, it must
discover not simply one, but the totality of actual conditions on the
basis of which all the determinations of that real actuality are actualized. For if all the conditions are not present, the actual is not possible.
A diverse multitude of actualities are put together under real possibility. That specific integration is thought as one, only because of an actuality which is distinct from any one of those integrated conditions.[27]

The concept 'real possibility' is highly complex, requiring a more
thorough speculative exploration. On the one hand, since the content
is an actual in one respect, and a possible in another, the sense of
'possible' is purely formal—it is that which does not contradict itself.
On the other hand, as the totality of conditions for one actuality, it
must be such that these conditions can be integrated without contradiction. Both formally and with respect to specific determinations, it
is that which does not contradict itself.

Further considerations, however, complicate the picture. For
reflection on the multiplicity that is inherent in real possibility distinguishes formally the different conditions. Each condition, as self-identical and immediately actual, is distinct from the others. As such it
stands over against the others. But then it is contradictory to say that
together they are *the* one possibility. Using the purely formal sense of
'possibility' as self-identical, it is not possible for a variety of different
conditions to be one. This strange conclusion follows not only from
formal considerations, but also from material considerations of real
possibility as a totality of conditions. A set of conditions is called the
real possibility of an actual because, when brought together, the multiplicity will be cancelled, and indeed collapse, as possibility. It *cannot*
maintain itself as many. In other words, it is *not possible* for all the
conditions to be integrated as a totality and still be simply possible.
For when all the conditions of something are present, it becomes actual. Indeed, the actuality as a thing with many properties is itself nothing else but this integration of its conditions.

On the one hand, a set of conditions is not the real possibility of a
thing unless all the conditions are present. On the other hand, when
all the conditions are present, the thing is no longer simply possible,
but actual. Indeed, the paradox is even stronger than this. Real possibility is that which, to be possible, contradicts itself neither formally
nor materially. Yet real possibility can be a simple self-identity neither
formally nor materially. Reflection on real possibility shows that it is
not possible to be both a *real* possibility of an actuality, and yet distinct from the actuality as possibility.[28]

When we recall all the steps through which we have moved in explicating real possibility, we discover a double process of cancelling. In the first place, the immediate actuality of the possible is cancelled as significant, and it is seen primarily as the possibility of another—as what that other is in itself. But in the second place we have now seen that its character as possible cannot be maintained. At the very point where it is really possible as the condition for another, it ceases to be possibility and becomes the resultant actual. Its possibility is cancelled in turn. The resultant actuality *is* the immediate being of real possibility.

As a result of speculative reflection it has become impossible to distinguish possibility and actuality. In the earlier discussion, where possibility was simple self-identity, the opposite of what was actual was also possible. Here, however, once all the conditions which make a thing possible are present, nothing else is possible. The actuality of these conditions is simply their actuality *as* conditions. But that actuality *of* the possible cannot now be distinguished from what is actualized *by* the possible.

When reflective thought turned to that possibility that is the ground of real actuality, it began by distinguishing the one from the other. But in the last analysis, having worked through all the speculative implications, it can no longer draw any clear distinctions at all. Simply as one condition among many, something cannot be a *real* possibility at all. As the totality of conditions, it can only arbitrarily be distinguished from what was to be grounded. Thought reaches the conclusion that the distinction between real possibility and real actuality can no longer be maintained. They have collapsed into a unity, which must now have its speculative sense explained.[29]

3. What is really possible in any complete sense *must* be actual. As that possibility that can do nothing else but become actual, it is necessary. This sense of 'necessity' is different from the earlier, formal, one. For there we saw that the contingent actuality which is both grounded and groundless is other than formal possibility per se. Here, however, real possibility is itself the necessity. "Under these conditions and circumstances," we say, "nothing else can follow." The distinction between real possibility and necessity is only apparent. When we say that something is really necessary, we include in that necessity all the content that constitutes and characterizes that something—that content originally included in the determinate sense of 'real possibility'.[30]

Real necessity is relative. It is based upon a presupposition, which is itself contingent. By this Hegel is not simply making the obvious point that our reflection on the implications of the meaning of 'contingency' has led us to this sense of 'real necessity', so that the former is the premise for the reflective procedure. Rather it is implicit in the content of the discussion itself. We began by thinking the concept 'real actuality'—immediate, but determinate reality. Real necessity concerns the relation between real possibility as condition, and this real actuality as conditioned. It presupposes, but is indifferent to, the specific determinations of whatever is so related. On the one hand, such content is the condition for understanding this concept; on the other, what that content is specifically is irrelevant. Whatever it is, it could have been otherwise. The only thing required is that it be a possible content in the simple formal sense of self-identity. As actual, it could have been other than itself. Indeed it is a contingent matter what content real actuality is given. Given that content, however, understanding will show that it *had to* be actual because of the total set of conditions.[31]

One cannot think of real necessity, then, without presupposing contingency. The relation is necessary but the content is contingent. Because of real possibility A, B must become actual. But the nature of the necessity is contingent on the specific determinations of A.

Not only is the content of the necessary relation contingent, but so is the relation itself. For the distinction between real possibility and the resultant actual is the result of reflection on that actual. But that reflective distinction is itself contingent and not inevitable. What thought distinguishes as the real possibility of an actual is not itself determined with necessity. Both in terms of content and form, real necessity presupposes contingency.

What we have, then, is a unity of necessity and contingency. Contingency is implicit in real necessity in so far as it is determinate and in so far as it requires, as a necessary condition, the reflective distinction between possibility and actuality.[32]

To understand 'real necessity' requires the distinction between real possibility and its actualization, even though this distinction cannot be maintained. Just as, however, thought moved from contingency to formal necessity by shifting the stress from the implicit relation of explicitly distinct terms to the explicit integration of implicit distinctions, so here understanding can collapse into a unity those moments that constitute real necessity. When thought no longer makes explicit distinctions between real possibility and real actuality, it takes the actual in its totality. Whatever is actual is simply actual, for the reference to a distinct possibility that grounds it is no longer appropriate. What thought now thinks is an actuality that has no external possibility in terms of which it is conditioned. Since there is no other, relative to which it becomes actual, it is absolute actuality.[33]

Absolute Necessity

(1) The logical demand to understand drives us further. To advance, however, we must recall our earlier conclusions. In the first section, the contingent, as both grounded and groundless, could not be distinguished from the formally necessary. In the second section, real necessity, both in content and in form, is contingently determined. These two moments come together in thought into a contingency that is necessary, and a necessity that is contingent. When these distinctions, however, are integrated into one thought, what results is the total complex of actuality. When we endeavour to understand precisely the ground of this actuality, there is no distinct possibility to which we can turn. This means that it is intrinsically necessary. It is absolutely actual.[34]

(2) Absolute actuality, then, has no possibility that is other than, or distinct from, its actuality. Its ground is its necessity. Yet understanding still asks the question: why? Since it can now not talk of formal self-identity, nor can it distinguish some actual from those others that render it possible, it can only inquire why there is anything at all. The ground that is sought in this question is empty of all content, for all determinate possibilities have collapsed into the absolutely actual. Therefore there is no answer to this reflective question. It is completely contingent that there be anything at all. It could have been absolutely otherwise.

When dialectic leads us to this possibility, no longer does it think the formal possibility of simple self-identity, nor indeed the real possibility of conditions. It is the possibility which reason entertains when it confronts the actual as necessary and absolute. But such possibilities can either remain a pure possibility with no actualization at all, or become the possibility of what is, in fact, actual. There is no reason why it should be the one rather than the other.

We are again faced with a speculative tension. What is absolutely actual is intrinsically necessary, yet it is completely contingent. On the one hand it is grounded in necessity because there is no distinct possibility to which we can turn. On the other hand it is grounded in absolute possibility which is independent of any reference to the actual.[35]

(3) This speculative contradiction requires resolution and explanation. Since there is no further external point of reference to provide such an explanation, understanding must reconsider the earlier argument in light of this new development. The concept of absolute actuality was the result of collapsing the distinctions in the concept of real necessity. The latter distinguished between real possibilities and the resultant actualities. Only on the basis of this distinction does real

necessity become possible. Since this distinction was collapsed into the concept of absolute actuality, it is implicit within it. What is thus hidden in the concept of absolute actuality needs now to be brought to light. The distinction between possible and actual is reintroduced, not as a relation of contrary opposites where both cannot be present at the same time, but as a relation of sub-contraries whose meanings are distinct and different, but which are yet explicitly related within a larger universe of discourse. In place of the earlier moves of thought which first treated the distinctions as explicit, and the relations as only implicit, and then shifted to collapsing the distinctions into an explicit unity, understanding now recognizes the necessity of taking both the distinctions and the relation as components of the meaning of the concept. On the one hand, the two moments of possibility and actuality are distinguished as the negation of each other; on the other, this negative relation is negated to reaffirm the unity.[36]

This new content of thought is what is actual, period. No longer do we contrast immediate or formal actuality with reflective considerations of its logical possibility. Nor do we distinguish determinate actuality from its real conditions. Nor indeed do we think of absolute actuality as simply necessary in itself. We are, instead, thinking of the actual as it actually is. We distinguish actuals which are real possibilities from that which they actualize. Indeed, the determinations that are actually present result from the internal relations by which the distinctions between actual and possible are both constituted as distinct and then related as part to whole. In other words, possibility is established as the opposite of the actual through the reflective determination of distinctions within the actual itself.

This process by which reflection distinguishes the possible from the actual mediates and grounds the actual. It renders the actual possible. The distinction and its resolution actualize and render determinate what the actual is implicitly. It is its *possibility* in a final and preeminent sense. Instead of thinking about absolute possibilities, understanding individuates the mediating process by which the actual determines itself.[37]

Thus understanding shows that 'the actual', as we are now thinking the term, constitutes itself as determinate by means of the relation in which possibility grounds actuality, and actuality is grounded by possibility. At the same time it generates that relation as the explicit form of its implicit character. As that which constitutes its own ground—as self-constituting—it is absolutely necessary. Thus absolute necessity gives rise to contingency as the ground of its own necessity. For it is contingent which moments are distinguished, separated and repelled from its actuality as its own conditions. Nonetheless, whatever moments are thus rendered determinate, it is necessary that they thereby become the means to its absolute self-determination. Without these contingent, determinate moments, absolute necessity could not be established as necessary. This play of countervailing forces determines the actual to be necessary by annulling, even while establishing, contingency. It generates, even as it transcends, the repelling moment of contrast and counterthrust. This necessity is necessity absolute. For it alone establishes the absolute necessity of contingency.[38]

With that, our assigned task has been accomplished. Contingency itself has been shown to be necessary without qualification.

Necessity as thus defined, however, is blind. There is no reason or purpose for the way in which it determines itself. Only where the necessity is taken up into an explicitly teleological perspective will it become the basis of freedom as intentional self-determination. But that is beyond the scope of this paper.

Conclusion

A few comments may be in order regarding the necessity of Hegel's method. You will recall that, at the beginning of the chapter, it was suggested that Hegel's logic develops through the process of thinking: "the careful *understanding* of determinate, positive characteristics; the *dialectical* implications of that determination; and reflection that integrates these specific contrary terms into a *speculative,* inclusive unity." These procedures took us initially, in a simple dialectic, from the most primitive sense of actuality through possibility as its opposite to the reflective integration of the two in contingency and formal necessity. These processes were themselves submitted to reflective scrutiny, producing the speculative concepts of real actuality, real possibility, and relative necessity. Understanding this result showed how all of the various components were to be integrated into a sense of necessity absolute.

Where lies the necessity of the movement? The answer can be suggested in three stages. In the first place, the concept with which we began, 'actuality', is a general concept. It is used to characterize all that is. But as first present in thought it is immediate and indeterminate. Rendering it determinate leads us into its dialectical implications: 'actual' always leads to 'possible' although the sense of those terms becomes more specific as we proceed through the various stages. Each of the terms is partial. When they are considered in themselves, apart from their context, their inherent limitations clash with the universality of that which they were to define. So in the second place, speculative reflection looks for what is essential in the reciprocal relation between actual and possible, only to discover that here too its conclusions shift from one contrary to another. In the third place, then, understanding explores how the various moments interact within the integrated unity: how the original characterization of actuality is rendered possible, and how the possibility in turn constitutes its necessity. In other words, each stage of the process is a necessary moment of its full, determinate development.

LOGIC APPLIED

VI

Challenge to Hegel:
Contraries and Contradictories
in Schelling's Late Philosophy

In the year 1841, the sixty-six-year-old Schelling was installed in the chair of philosophy at Berlin. Because the new king of Prussia wanted someone with sufficient authority to combat the influence of Hegel, he supported the appointment. As crown prince he had been concerned about liberal and subversive elements in Hegel's political philosophy. Once in power, he chose an associate of Hegel's youth to lead the attack, a man who had disappeared from the intellectual scene just as Hegel's star was beginning to rise. Although Schelling and Hegel were collaborators in the years that led up to the *Phenomenology of Spirit*, Schelling had not been converted to dialectical philosophy. Indeed, in lectures on the history of philosophy given in Munich during the years after Hegel's death, he challenged its rationality. The move from the logic of pure thought to a philosophy of nature was unjustified. For Schelling there could be no logical bridge between transcendental idealism (as he had called the a priori system taken over from Fichte and Kant) and the theory which expressed the inherent structure of nature. They are two quite different disciplines, of quite a different order. When Hegel moved from one to the other, then, he was violating a fundamental logical principle, first enunciated by Aristotle. He was passing over into another genus—from thought to reality. The image that sprang to Schelling's mind was one vividly expressed by Lessing. Between these two—thought and reality—lay an "ugly broad ditch."[1]

Schelling's challenge to Hegel concerned the nature of thinking and reasoning. He accused his predecessor in the chair at Berlin of

55

committing a logical fallacy: Reason could not initiate a philosophy of nature simply on the basis of its own self-contained structure. And that fallacy vitiated the system.

Yet Schelling himself was not content to remain with a rational philosophy. The lectures in Berlin, although published under the titles "Philosophy of Mythology" and "Philosophy of Revelation,"[2] argued that pure reason could produce only a negative philosophy, one which spelled out the possibility of things, but was impotent in establishing their actuality. In contrast, Schelling advanced a new type: positive philosophy, whose task it is to be a philosophy of existence. No less than Hegel, then, did he maintain the two disciplines, earlier called transcendental philosophy and philosophy of nature. His disagreement focused on the process of reasoning itself.

While Hegel's logic and philosophy have been subjected to any number of critical examinations,[3] Schelling's thought has remained relatively unnoticed. Yet because his critique of Hegel centres on the invalidity of the ultimate dialectical transition, it poses a central question: What does it mean to be logical? His own system develops by providing an answer. Indeed, reflections on reason and reasoning offer justification for splitting philosophy into two. Since Schelling alone was both precursor and subsequent critic of Hegel, these reflections may well throw light on the nature of reasoning and how it can be applied to the natural world.

Establishing the First Principle

In his Berlin lectures Schelling first turns his attention to the philosophy of pure reason. His question is an important one: How can reason establish its first principles? Kant's transcendental philosophy had assumed not only the knowledge achieved by the science of its day; it also reflected on this knowledge and discriminated between its constituent structure and its contingent content. Kant's successors were not content simply to use such reflection; they needed to justify the role reason plays in the process. To be sure that transcendental reflection be logical and necessary, it must first be examined. Fichte had undertaken this task in the first three principles of the *Science of Knowledge.*[4] In his late philosophy Schelling reviewed the procedure involved.

To reach first principles one cannot use deduction. For deduction moves from a principle or universal to a particular or instance. It applies a rule to a case. Since first principles have to be the most universal ones, from which everything else is to be derived, we cannot appeal to anything more ultimate to justify their status deductively.

Yet philosophy requires logical justification for each one of its steps. Since the starting point cannot be established through deduction, the only alternative for Schelling is its contrary, induction. Rather than moving from universal to particular, this inference moves from particular to universal.[5]

However, the simple disjunction, deduction/induction, hides a difficulty. What is normally called induction collects a number of particulars from experience, and then tries to discover in them a shared universal. But experience is bedevilled with contingency. Not only is it a matter of chance what, in a particular, is encountered by the senses; the subject is also not governed by strict necessity when it draws its conclusion. Because of this uncertainty normal induction is an inappropriate means for arriving at the first principles of a rational science.

However, the premises for an induction need not be the particulars given in sense experience. The inference can start from particular thoughts and concepts—ways by which we characterize whatever is. In the act of thinking these thoughts, we become aware of features that are contingent. This awareness of contingency is a way of cancelling, or negating, the necessity of these thoughts. Since they can be "not thought," they cannot be the ultimate principles which are to be the conclusion of the inductive process. Through such particular acts of thinking, one may arrive at a feature or thought that cannot be "not thought"—something the act of thinking cannot cancel. This is the conclusion of the induction. As necessary (since its opposite is not a possible thought), it is a comprehensive universal. Yet it has been derived from particular acts of thinking.[6]

Basic to this type of induction are particular attempts to think the opposite of something. Reason is able to cancel its own content to negate whatever is presented to it. Its ultimate principles are those thoughts which it can*not negate* in this way.

The two negatives stressed in the previous sentence do not simply make a positive. For they are of a different order. The second is our rational ability to cancel or negate the content of thought. This does not annihilate absolutely its object. Rather, it takes that content as one side of a pair of contraries, both of which may be thought in disjunction, though not in conjunction. Through disjunction, reason thinks the alternative contrary to the one originally thought. Rational negation uses this pattern of contraries, in which each side of a disjunction is possible and *can* be thought.

The first negation is different. Reason comes up against a particular content which it cannot negate in the normal way. This incapacity is not a denial of the particular content, but a limitation inherent in the act of thinking itself. No matter how hard one tries to think this particular opposite, one is not able to do it. It is in no way an entertained possibility. "One must *actually* think to *experience* [the fact] that the contradictory is not thinkable."[7]

This appeal to actual fact is dangerous, however, since it indicates a subjective, or psychological, incapacity of the individual who is thinking. And subjectivity is notoriously variable. The risk involved does not dismay Schelling. For there are two sides to this particular incapacity. It is subjective, to be sure, but it is also the incapacity to think the negative of a certain principle. And the principle is universal. Reason is defined by its ability to reduce a universal to being one contrary moment within a disjunction—the disjunction being more universal than the original term. What cannot be so negated can only be that universal which is completely universal. It has no contraries. The counterpart of this objective structure is the subjective incapacity. And vice versa. Therefore the subjective fact provides the experimental evidence that the induction has reached its end.[8]

These two types of negation are reflected in the two negative particles to be found in Greek. The word *ou* is used primarily with the indicative mood in independent sentences; its counterpart *mē* is used with the subjunctive and the imperative, as well as in purposive and conditional clauses. The latter term, then, is used in those circumstances where the content denied remains a possibility. It can still be entertained rationally. To quote Aristotle: "what is non-being yet has the possibility of being."[9] By contrast, when *ou* is used, there is no suggestion that the content denied is still possible. It simply indicates a fact that it has not occurred.

The negation of content in the "inductive" process of reason is a conditional negation, one whose opposite is a possible thought, since that opposite was in fact present in the content originally thought. However, the incapacity of reason to think a contradiction is an indicative negation: its opposite does not remain as a possible thought; its opposite simply does not occur.

The two types of negation solve an apparent dilemma in the very concept of a first principle. On the one hand, it must be established rationally; on the other, subsequent principles and inferences must be derivable from it. In both operations, reason will function as a negating agent. Yet the way it functions will have to be different in each case.

Thus, for example, what Schelling calls *das Seinkönnende*—what can be—will be the first principle only if it is just not feasible to consider its opposite. However, a second principle can be derived only if reason, by conditionally negating the first, can show it to be only one disjunct of two—that it requires a complement or contrary to be complete. In other words, the ultimate first principle must be such that it both has, and has not, an appropriate contrary.

That itself appears to be contradictory, and thus unthinkable. The appearance can be shown to be misleading only because the two different types of negation are involved.

The ultimate principle first comes to be entertained through the use of conditional negation: What is could not be. The conditional form 'could' indicates that its non-being is yet something possible—non-being can be.

'Possibility' is an ambiguous term, however. It might mean certain conditions through which a physical event comes to be; it might mean coherence with a set of circumstances. Both define possibility with reference to something not possible but actual. In the most universal principle, however, this relativity must itself be cancelled. The most general sense of possibility is simply that something can be thought on its own, apart from all relation. Whatever can be so thought *can be*, at least in this most generic sense of possibility.

Does this mean that things which cannot be thought cannot be? Schelling does not draw this conclusion. As we shall see, this alternative possibility will become the basis for his positive philosophy. What he does claim is that the ultimate principle of *rational* philosophy must be thinkable. That is simply a tautology. This then leads to his further inferences: What can be thought can be, in the most general sense of possibility. And since thought can entertain the possibility of something that can be without being thinkable, it can acknowledge that the concept 'what can be' is more nearly universal than the concept 'what can be thought'.

He has not yet proven that 'what can be' is the ultimate first principle. This requires a further argument, involving once again the use of negation. Negation is already an inherent constituent of this concept. Aristotle has identified the possibility of being with the conditional negation of being. Thought began its search for ultimate principles with the actual world, which provides it with raw material. It moved from the actual to the possible through its exercise of conditional negation. 'Possibility,' then, has the negation of its contrary, 'actuality', as a constituent of its meaning.

The opposite of 'what can be' in its most comprehensive sense is not, then, simply 'what is', but rather 'that which neither is nor can be'. This negation cancels not only the possibility but also its derivation through negation from actuality. Such a negation can be expressed by placing the negative particle in front of the noun clause: 'not what can be'. But although this can be said or written, it simply cannot be thought. Reason finds that it cannot integrate the negation

with the term to be negated into a new single term. For reason's negation implies possibility, and it is this possibility that is to be negated.
Reason here encounters an indicative negation that marks the ultimate limits of thought. As such it has all the evidence it requires to
know that it has reached the most universal term from which it may
derive theoretical science.[10]

Deriving Other Principles

When Schelling turns around to develop the rational philosophy from
this first principle, he once again has only negation as a tool. This
time, however, he does not run up against an indicative incapacity to
reason. The specific contrary of 'what can be,' or the possible, is the
actual, or 'what is'. As its opposite and hence excluding possibility, it
is pure actuality or pure being. In that contrast, the first principle
itself becomes more precisely defined as pure possibility, excluding
actuality. These two terms have become particulars and exclusive disjuncts. By themselves, however, they are not sufficient to ground
rational philosophy. For the relation of pure otherness leaves no possibility of combining them so that further inferences can be made.
This impossibility points to a new contrary. We have as our first two
principles pure possibility and pure being. The third principle should
be neither the one nor the other. As other than both, and excluded
from them, it negates that which they share. In other words, it is the
opposite of that purity by which they exclude each other; the third
principle is the combination of possibility and being.[11]

We can now return to our earlier question: How can the first principle both have and not have an appropriate contrary? The answer
lies in the range of the negation. When establishing a principle as ultimate and universal, negation is applied to the whole concept. The
inductive search entails universalizing its content completely. The fact
that the most nearly universal does not have a contrary leads to the
indicative impossibility of negating, which shows that the ultimate
principle has been reached. On the other hand, the development from
the first principle is from a universal to its particular—a species of
deduction. Therefore negation is applied to that which specifically
distinguishes the ultimate principle: the concept of possibility. And in
the move to the third principle, the isolation of the two that prevents
conjunction is negated, not their complementary content.

As Schelling develops the negative philosophy it becomes clear
that there is a further range of meanings in the concept of possibility.
The first three principles do not actually exist. They are the possibili-

ties or potencies which underlie all experience. Even 'actuality' or 'pure being' remains a potency. Aware of this, reason can negate the moment of possibility in its content. It can consider what the various moments *would* be if they were not principles but if each were itself something that is. Every such move remains conditional, not indicative. Because the rational operation operates only with conditional negation, it never escapes the sphere of simple possibility, no matter how complex its constructions.

Pure thinking, then, cannot get beyond itself to existence. But it can reflect on its own structure and acknowledge this inherent limitation. In other words, rational philosophy can recognize that its framework of pure possibility needs to be complemented by the givens of existence. For only through experience will its structure of inherent necessity be shown to be true of the world.

In this, Schelling reproduces a fundamental conviction of Immanuel Kant: "It is indispensably necessary for the human understanding," wrote Kant in his *Critique of Judgement*, "to distinguish between the possibility and the actuality of things.... Such a distinction would not be given were there not requisite for knowledge two quite different elements, understanding for concepts and sensible intuition for objects corresponding to them."[12]

How is it possible for reason not simply to recognize its need for experience but to effect the conjunction of its possibility with given actuals?[13] That conjunction lies outside its capacity, since its capacity is defined by conditional negation. For Kant, sensible intuition is a given constituent of experience that analysis has distinguished from conceptual understanding. For Schelling, as for Fichte, the question is quite different: How can this analytic distinction itself be shown to be rational? Since Schelling's science, unlike Kant's critical philosophy, does not have experience as a source, how can it have experience as a companion?[14]

Schelling's answer is significant. Reason's awareness of its own limitation is displayed "as an *existamenon* in the proper sense, as something placed outside of itself that has lost itself, as a being no longer master of itself, because it is relieved of the power which it was, somewhat as a man with unruly desires forfeits the power of desiring, forfeits the will itself; thus it will appear as a will-less volition."[15]

Although this ecstasy is defined as the contrary of rational capacities ("it is relieved of the power which it was"), the subject who becomes ecstatic remains yet capable of reason. This moment thus involves a distinct type of negation. At first it appears to be simply conditional denial once again: what is not within reason's own capacity is still possible. But that possibility is only confirmed when the event occurs in fact. In ecstasy there is a conjunction of reason's possibility with the actuality of experience—of a conditional with an indicative.

Schelling captures this character with his phrase will-less volition (*ein willenloses Wollen*). As in all decisions there is a simple indicative; an action simply takes place. But in this decision the act does not respond to a particular rational intention. Indeed it is characterized as the contrary of any such intention, else reason could be charged with "cooking its evidence." At the same time, this moment is reached through the rational philosophy; it is acknowledged as its contrary. Conditional negation at this point cancels itself, even though this self-cancelling requires as its complement the simple positives of sense and experience.

Since the givens of experience are but the complement of reason's self-cancelling, they serve to instantiate the conditions and principles articulated by reason. Just as in Kant's philosophy intuition is formed by understanding, so here the givens which reason discovers in its ecstasy are formed by its own inherent capacity. This means, however, that reason can become aware of a limitation inherent in the negative philosophy. Because experience is structured by reason's categories, the actual world is known only through those categories. Experience is thus the way things appear, not necessarily the way they are. And in the most crucial sphere of life that appearance may simply be a wish fulfillment. When someone tries to act conscientiously, he or she discovers that this action is nevertheless immoral. Frustrated, one yearns for a reconciliation between what ought to be and what is. A rational projection molds one's perception of the world. But one is not satisfied here with a theory in which existence does no more than complement reason. One wants to know how things really are, apart from one's rational projections. One wants to know whether actual existence offers a real reconciliation.[16]

This marks the crisis of rational philosophy for Schelling. The human being, in this way radically finite, "drives me to the final despairing question: 'Why is there anything at all? Why is there not nothing?'"[17]

The Positive Philosophy

Nevertheless Schelling does not reject philosophy. On the contrary he proposes a different science, a positive philosophy, which would be the counterpart of the (Kantian) negative philosophy.

Schelling here presents himself with a dilemma. On the one hand, reason on its own cannot answer the "final despairing question." Yet on the other, the answer to that question cannot be arbitrary. It is, after all, a philosophical question, an asking why. And it expects an answer that is not only comprehensible, but has some element of inevitability. It needs to be justified. The question has arisen because someone has become aware of fallibility in the exercise of moral reason. And reliability cannot be re-established through any immediate assertion or simple conviction; it requires critical reflection. In other words, reason cannot be avoided.

Within rational philosophy we have found that reason can become ecstatic—it goes beyond itself. What thus lies beyond reason is nevertheless within the capacity of the reasoning being. This ecstatic contrary of reason is volition:

> The volition that is for us the beginning of another world, posited outside of the Idea, is something originating purely in itself, as a *cause of itself* in quite a different sense than that used by Spinoza concerning universal substance; for one can say of it only that it IS, not that it necessarily IS. In this sense it is what is primally contingent, the primal accident itself.[18]

Reason operates with a conditional negation. Only in the attempt to think the first principles of rational philosophy did it encounter the indicative negation of its own incapacity. This latter was not something intended; it was simply encountered as a fact in the present. At the same time, while the act of will is positive, it also has a negative side; the act of positing is an act of excluding. But unlike the conditional negation of reason, it is not determined by the possibility of the contrary. What is excluded simply does not occur; it has lost any chance of being possible. The will thus exercises an indicative rather than a conditional negation. What is decided simply is.

Through the will, Schelling writes, the self "turns into something individual, for this volition *is* just what is individual in it."[19] Willed decisions, therefore, are inescapably contingent and particular. If reason is impotent to develop a positive philosophy because it is limited to pure possibility, the will is ambiguous and at times perverse. In some way the universality and necessity of reason needs to complement the individuality and actuality of will.

At the moment of reason's ecstasy, the two come together. Within the rational philosophy, reason has opened itself to experience; the actuals of sense intuition are correlated with its own principles. For a positive philosophy, however, one can neither start from the rational principles, nor from experience already structured in their terms. The ecstasy of reason needs to be directed, not to that which can be experienced, but to an existent that is beyond all experience; for it is to be the first principle of all reality. To be open simply to that which is relatively other would once again land us in the ambiguities of finite existence. At the beginning of positive philosophy, reason opens itself to that which is its absolute other.

At the same time the affirmation of will cannot exclude all but one rationally proposed option. It must exclude *all* possibility whatsoever. It will refer to that which is actual prior to *any* conditions, *any* potencies, and indeed *any* logical principles. Any possibility comes into being, as it were, with its actuality; this entity is the cause of itself in a preeminent sense. To insure this universality in its act of exclusion, the will cannot be left to its own contingent and arbitrary operation. It requires the generalizing capacity of reason.

In union with the ecstasy of reason, then, the will may posit pure existence: a 'that' without any 'what'. Freed of rational possibility, this would be an existence that is *un*conditioned, *un*premeditated (*unvordenklich*). As cause of itself, this embodies preeminently the structure of the will; for volition, too, "is something which originates purely in itself."[20] The ecstatic union of reason with the will is thus not simply a subjective achievement of an inquiring philosopher. Rather, in the ecstatic moment the subject conforms to the object of reference—with the unconditioned existent that is posited. At this point, like is "knowing" like.

Schelling is not suggesting that the *existence* of this unpremeditated existent is created in the ecstasy of reason. Such a conclusion would be self-contradictory. Rather the self here *refers to* pure existence and at the same time wills to affirm it as the first principle of a different kind of philosophy. In the same way that rational philosophy refers to an alien experience, the self indicates unpremeditated existence. But, lacking the conditions provided by a priori rational principles, this act of reference is an unconditioned positing by the will, a *causa sui*.[21] This first principle is thus not a rational thought. It is something "preposited"—in German, a *Vorstellung*. The combination of reason's exhaustive self-knowledge and of will's exclusive and indicative negation ensures that this prepositing is neither arbitrary nor subjective. It can be confidently accepted as a principle that is not otherwise.

Reasoning per posterius

Simply to preposit unconditioned existence could be the end of all philosophy. For reason has accepted it as that which is absolutely other than all conceptual possibility. As such, there is nothing inherent in this prepositing that opens the way to intellectual development, nor to any explanation of the ambiguities and perversities of the world. Schelling does not accept this implication, however. In the first place, the unconditioned existent has not been preposited as a first principle in an antirational way. Reason's ecstasy continues to be a function of a reasonable being, even though it has become identified with its contrary, the indicative affirmation of will. In the second place, in experience we find actual conditioned existents, which have a prior possibility, or 'what'. If reason were to take these two givens, present as diverse moments of its own ecstasy, and set them within a single perspective, it might thus from the synthesis derive principles in accordance with which the two are related. This possibility opens the way for philosophy once again.

The first consequence of such a synthesis is the recognition of a distinct order. While the unconditioned can remain quite unrelated to anything else, the conditioned presupposes a relation to its condition. That conditioning agent is itself conditioned (in which case the question reoccurs) or unconditioned. Further, either something unconditioned occurs somewhere in the regress, or the series is infinite and itself unconditioned. In both cases conditioned existence presupposes a derivative relation to something unconditioned.

This move does not resolve our dilemma, however. For existence and the will are, as we have seen, contingent and accidental. How can reason explore the relation between conditioned and unconditioned without falling prey to mere opinion and chance? Either it will do so on the basis of some character discovered in contingent existence— thus retracing the route followed by the negative philosophy—or it will be condemned to arbitrary contingency in ascribing any character at all to the unpremeditated existent.

Schelling grasps both horns of the dilemma. Reason does reproduce in a way the stages of negative philosophy, yet its conclusions are contingent. The contingency, however, does not concern the content of its conclusions—the 'what'—but only whether it exists in fact; while the constant reference to existence modifies the description of the rational principle.

Reason is essentially conditional. At this point in the argument, being conditional is no longer a limitation but a strength, for reason can proceed hypothetically. Building on the ordered relation of unconditioned and conditioned, reason can consider what would be the case if the preposited unconditioned *were* the ground of all experienced existence. Using the same combination of the indicative inability to think a contradiction and the conditional ability to think con-

traries that was used in establishing the first principles of the negative
philosophy, reason spells out the inherent nature which the absolutely unconditioned would have *if* it were, contingently, to be the condition for a derivative world, that is, if it were to be God. Then it can
turn to the way God would have to function *if* God were to activate
that nature and actually create. Subsequently, reason can describe the
nature of the world that would be so created. *If* this creation would
involve freedom, the effects of exercising freedom could be shown;
and *if* the freedom were to be exercised, the manner of tackling its
consequences could likewise be shown.

In each of these moves, reason cannot provide complete descriptions. It may, however, through conditional negation, divide the
range of possible consequences into two contrary general principles.
Each of these may then be tentatively conjoined with all the conditions governing that stage of the argument to determine which set of
conjunctions cannot be integrated in thought. The other set thus
becomes conditionally necessary. At the very least, reason has shown
that "nothing prevents" its coming to be.[22]

Since conditionally negating to specify contraries and the indicative impossibility of thinking contradictories are the same in this procedure as in the negative philosophy, it is not surprising that developments in the positive philosophy closely resemble the principles of
the earlier, negative, philosophy. Only the fact that they are tentative
rather than necessary appears to distinguish them.

Schelling moves from being tentative to being positive through
reference to actual existence. The positive philosopher asks: Within
experience itself does one encounter the features specified in reason's
hypothesis? This is not strictly an argument a posteriori. One does not
move from the particulars of experience to an inductive generalization. Schelling calls it a proof *per posterius*. The consequent of a hypo-
thetical statement is experienced as true. A priori reasoning has
already shown that one or other of two contraries is necessarily
implied by the one condition that is in question. That condition had
been in doubt because both contraries could have been false. The fact
that one has been experienced as true thus establishes the truth of the
condition. "Through its results is the prior known."[23]

At each stage in the positive philosophy, then, the following logical pattern occurs. Two givens that have a definite logical order are
acknowledged. The first principle plus whatever has already been
derived from it *per posterius* has a logical priority; it is a possible condition. Experience as determinate and conditioned is logically posteri-
or. The task is to find a middle term which is both the immediate consequent of the condition and sufficiently determinate to entail a

difference in the actual world. When that difference is found independently to hold true in the world, the truth of the middle term is confirmed, and it can then be added to the set of logically prior terms.[24]

What about the independent evidence of experience? At the earli-
est stages of the positive philosophy this presents little problem. The
questions to be asked are quite general: Do we experience conditioned existence at all? Does the world have a pattern of determination in which possibles become actuals—or causes have effects? The
further one proceeds, however, the more difficult the question
becomes: Has the exercise of human freedom opened up a range of
consequences that men and women no longer can control? Has God,
the unconditioned agent, acted to bring these uncontrollable forces
under control? It would appear that the answers to these questions
will not provide the necessary independence. Experience will not simply offer its evidence in an immediate intuition; the evidence will be
interpreted—and the interpretation will reflect the original hypothesis. By framing its questions so precisely, reason will structure the
way nature and history are intuited.

Schelling claims that philosophy need not necessarily beg the
question. The exercise of human freedom creates history. The immediate participants in history reflect on their actions together with the
consequences of those actions. This reflection distinguishes contingent particulars from essential themes. As these themes are shared
and communicated from generation to generation they acquire a comprehensive flavor, reflecting the way a culture views the universe. In
other words, the religious thoughts of men and women reveal the
central themes of their historical existence. Mythology and revelation—which have been handed down from generation to generation,
and are recorded in written texts and cultural traditions—provide the
independent evidence required by the method. The task of positive
philosophy is not to impose its framework on these traditions, but to
expose their inherent structure, seeing whether that structure confirms or not the middle term proposed a priori.

As a result, Schelling's late system does not simply present the
contrasting methods of negative and positive philosophy. Much more
of its space is devoted to a description of ancient mythologies and of
Christian doctrine—so much so that it has been published under the
titles *Philosophy of Mythology* and *Philosophy of Revelation*. The titles are
misleading. For Schelling's purpose is not to philosophize about
mythology and revelation: not to draw inductive generalizations from
them, or to reinterpret them speculatively so that they form a single
theoretical framework. He intends to describe them, nothing more.
The description is then to confirm or disconfirm his a priori hypothe-

sis. Because the positive philosophy has abandoned a purely rational approach, it must rely on the detail of such description to test its more complicated hypotheses. In this way philosophy has become but one component of a larger discipline that includes history.

Conclusion

We have now completed our description of Schelling's philosophical method in his 1841 lectures. The question with which we are left is whether or not he is subject to his own criticism of Hegel: In his move from a rational to a positive philosophy, does he pass over into another genus?

Certainly Schelling does not want to identify the will with reason. The former simply concerns existence. It acts or not: there is no third possibility. When it does act, a 'that' comes into being. It is this characteristic of the will that makes it an appropriate agent both for prepositing an existential first principle and for referring without presupposition to the givens of experience. For existence and nonexistence are contradictories, not contraries.

By contrast, reason reflects on possibilities and principles. Its negation does not produce a contradictory, but only a contrary: A term and its opposite may not both be true, but they could both be false. They are therefore species of a universal, embodying not contradiction but a type of disjunction. Because all of reason's content could be false, it is unable to establish any 'that'. Its sphere covers only the 'what': nature, determination, and quality.

But although the will with its focus on the 'that' contrasts with reason and its 'what', they are not of different genera. For they are disjunctive contraries of the same subject. The self can refer and preposit, or it can reflect. These two postures are not contradictories, for the self could simply not exist, in which case both alternatives would be false. In other words, reason and the will are different capacities of a single being—species, in a sense, of a single genus. Through this more comprehensive context they become the two complementary moments of a single reflective discipline. An act of will has consequences; it conditions its product. Therefore reason's conditionals become appropriate, and the individuality of existence can be explained. On the other hand, reason can apply its operation of conditional negation to itself and become ecstatic. Open to the 'thats' of pure reference, it can verify the truth of its own theoretical principles.

Thus each of the contraries completes what is lacking in its opposite; there is no illegitimate jump into an alien genus. Even though pure reason cannot establish existence and pure will cannot produce explanations, each can play its appropriate role in a more comprehensive perspective.

Because thought and will are of the same genus, the essential nature of willed existence can be anticipated through reason. Whether that essence exists or not may be contingent; but its central content will not be. Its possibility can be projected by a priori reflection.

In this, Schelling's theory contrasts with that of his antagonist, Hegel. For Hegel, reflection on the possibilities of existence is not prior, but subsequent, to existence. The first rational moment is an immediate transition. And that transition presents reason with a fact which only then can be explained. Unreflective existence is thus not alien to thought, but a moment in its own process. For this reason, Hegel argues that contingency is necessary. It is not only the presupposition of any reflection, it is also the inevitable product of any comprehensive theory. For the immediate reactions to a theory cannot be exhaustively anticipated by that theory, and such unanticipated moments turn out to be of crucial significance in subsequent reflection.[25]

This pattern, inherent in logic, is the same as those found in willed action and in the philosophy of nature. The will acts immediately and produces contingencies. Precisely those contingencies—not only as fact but also as specific content—provide the givens which theory has to comprehend. And Hegel does not deduce a philosophy of nature from his logical principles as Schelling had thought. He uses reflection to comprehend the distinctive features, contingent as they are, discovered by natural science. In other words, whereas an outline of the essential nature of the universe and human history can be projected a priori by Schelling, for Hegel reason is powerless until the actual world has had its day; philosophy about the real world is an a posteriori discipline. And whereas in Schelling contingency is accidental and may be overlooked in a philosophical discipline, in Hegel contingency provides the essential content of all reflection.

Neither Hegel nor Schelling ultimately commits the fallacy of passing over to another genus. For thought and reality are not absolute contradictories; they are contraries within a single perspective. Where the two philosophers differ is in the status of contingency. Contingent content is for Schelling unessential; for Hegel it is critical.

In other words, the King of Prussia had chosen well. Schelling's philosophy was essentially conservative. In principle (that is, from the standpoint of reason) there is nothing new under the sun; the only question is whether reason's eternal possibilities actually exist. If the necessity of contingency in Hegel's philosophy was subversive, here was a safe antidote. Unfortunately it was not effective. For Søren Kierkegaard heard these lectures and went out to write philosophical essays that placed contradiction at their core—marking the end of all rational science.[26] Friedrich Engels, equally dismayed, met Marx and, together with him, advocated revolution—the creation of a world that would be genuinely new. The rational thesis of Schelling was not simply conditionally negated to produce a contrary. It was rejected—and in that rejection contingency was accorded essential significance.

VII

Is Hegel a Rationalist or an Empiricist?

The question appears redundant. Here is a philosopher who starts his system with a "science of logic" and derives from it a philosophy of nature and a philosophy of spirit. In the preface to one of his last works he notoriously claimed that the rational is real and the real rational.[1] Reason reigns supreme, masquerading as nature or providence. Indeed Hegel has been accused of having deduced the (wrong) number of planets. Even to suggest that he is an heir of the empiricists seems out of place.

Yet the signs are not unequivocal. For Hegel's reason does not obviously match with that of Descartes or Leibniz. He is uncomfortable with "clear and distinct" as a way of classifying ideas; and contradiction does not lead into absurdity, but into a dialectic whose dance step is difficult to decipher.

At the same time, those who have pondered the pages of the *Phenomenology* have frequently come away impressed by the sensitivity with which Hegel captures human experience: not only the confident assertions of sense knowledge but also the disconcerted realization that experience does not provide us with what it promised. He makes us aware that the vaunted tabula rasa of the empiricists conveniently ignores those moments of consciousness that do not conform to its dogma: the continuities of space and time, the discriminations between essential and inessential, the despair when confronted with decay and death. By sensitively identifying moments of consciousness usually overlooked, Hegel has been more empirical than the empiricists.

Perhaps, then, our original question is not so much redundant as irrelevant. The traditional dichotomy between rationalists and empiricists becomes pointless when applied to Hegel. For all that the debates between Leibniz and Locke, and Hume and Wolff, dominated the

71

eighteenth century, they have no bearing on this intellectual descendant of Fichte and Schelling, who developed his philosophy during the early decades of the nineteenth. Hegel is working in an altogether different milieu.

That response, however, simply introduces a further dichotomy—this time between centuries. For all of the differences in Hegel's use of the word *reason*, for all of the differences in what is considered empirical data, there is nonetheless a continuity. Hegel is an heir of the antitheses that divided Europe during the Enlightenment.

So to answer our question we must uncover the connections that bind Hegel to his predecessors, the continuities as well as the differences. And our answer may well throw light on what this philosopher was actually about.

Rationalism appealed to the self-evidence of clear and distinct ideas. But its strongest weapon was the *reductio ad absurdum*. Showing that a claim led to self-contradictions established the truth of its contradictory. Without any appeal to experience it was thus possible to reach truths about the world.

Kant appealed to arguments of this sort in developing his antinomies. In warranting their validity, however, he showed something else. *Reductios* can themselves produce unavoidable contradictions: The world had a beginning in space and time; the world is infinite in space and time. All events in the world are necessitated by causes; some events are free and uncaused. Such rationalist arguments, he concluded, involve a relationship between ideas, but need not apply to the world of experience. And when they go beyond experience they establish no truth.

Hegel, however, turns things around. "Everything is contradictory," he says. And he makes dialectical contradictions the way station on the road to truth.

Differences start out simply as diverse, distinguishing things in a way that has no relation at all to their continuity and similarity. But then the way they are alike is opposed to the way they are unlike; it is not simply a diversity but an opposition. Since the similarities and differences are now not just creations of thought but characteristics of the thing itself, the opposition becomes a contradiction. What differentiates contradicts what is continuous.

This is certainly true of thoughts. Ideas are rendered clear and distinct (Hegel prefers the term "determinate") when their limits are defined. Yet they arise out of, and dissolve into, the continuity of thinking through a process of derivation and implication. Each idea involves the contradiction between being an individual and being an instance of the general.

But it is also true of nature and history. A single rock is continuous with granite, yet its difference creates the "contradiction" through which it wears away its fellows. A dog lives as a moment in the vital continuity that extends through generations, but it dies because it is a separate and distinct entity. Capitalism is the progressive result of feudalism and mercantilism, but effectively destroys its predecessors because of its differences.

Contradictions, then, are not simply absurd; they emerge when we identify carefully the various characteristics of natural things and historical events. Nonetheless Hegel's intention is not "to operate freely with all contradictions," as Popper claims.[2] For he is also prepared to use contradiction as a reason for rejecting a theory. As our examples have suggested, contradictions are the way things come to their end. An idea passes over to its implication; a rock is ground to dust; a dog dies; the capitalism of bourgeois society requires the intervention of the state.

In other words, contradictions are both necessary and contingent. They emerge from a determinate understanding of what things are, yet they are also self-destructive. They are themselves contradictory. Since they are thus inherently transient, they cannot provide a basis for understanding or explaining the world. It is the contradictions in logic and in the world that press thought to seek explanations or provide grounds.

As in rationalism, then, contradictions are stations on the way to truth. But Hegel diverges from his predecessors on the nature of the truth that results. It lies not in the contradictory of the thesis from which the contradiction is derived, but in the ground or explanation of the contradiction—the intellectual framework of continuity and discreteness that shows why the general requires its discrete moments, why the discrete moments frustrate and destroy the general, and why that destruction itself confirms and transforms the general. Comprehensive theory is the truth that emerges from the self-destructive transience of contradiction.

If contradictions are stations on the way to truth not because they are to be rejected but because they are to be transformed, then contradictions are not to be avoided, but welcomed. Indeed they are inevitable, characterizing thought, nature, and society. How, then, do they develop? They cannot simply be postulated through an arbitrary whim or designing scheme.

The answer to this question requires several stages. First we shall consider how contradictions arise in thought; then how they emerge in nature and history.

As the rationalists noted, rational thought involves getting our concepts clear and distinct. Concepts need to be made precise and defined; their appropriate genus as well as the specific difference need to be identified. This, suggests Hegel, is the task of understanding: particularizing concepts until they are fully determinate, identifiable, and fixed individuals.

What the rationalists did not notice was that every such move to precision triggers an intellectual transition. Thought passes over to something different. The empiricists called this 'association', and suggested that it was a habit of mind nurtured by constant conjunction in experience. They, however, failed to make an important distinction. Some transitions are derived from experience, as when we think of butter, having been reminded of bread. Others, however, are not from one experienced object or quality to another, but from one concept to another. Thought moves from 'something' to 'other'; from 'actual' to 'possible'; from 'one' to 'many'; from 'substance' to 'accidence'; from 'thing' to 'property'; from 'essence' to 'existence'; from 'finite' to 'infinite'. Not only are these transitions not derived from experience, but empirical associations presuppose them. They move from the thought of something *actual* (such as bread) to some other property that is *possible* (such as buttered). The intellectual transitions of thought provide the schemata within which the associations derived from constant conjunction function.

Those schematic transitions generate the contradictions of logic. For each involves a move to a different concept that is not simply diverse, but also opposed to the original. This opposition has not been imposed by arbitrary thought, but has developed implicitly out of the original concept. A contradiction appears once a fixed concept is taken together with its implied opposite. They require each other even though they are antithetical.

The crucial question, then, centers on these transitions of thought we call implications. How do they arise? What makes them inevitable?

It is not enough to say that they are a means to the end of comprehensively understanding the ground. Nor is it enough to say that they are necessary because of the specific definition of the original concept. Although both answers are acceptable as far as they go, they do not explain why thought makes just this move and no other. Other comprehensive results were possible. Thought could have remained content with a single concept rendered fully determinate.

No such external justification for the move we call implication is possible. These transitions of thought simply happen. This is the way rational thought functions. And the task of Hegel's logic is to purify the transitions in consciousness from all empirical accretions so that these basic movements and transitions can be identified.

In other words, at the center of logical science is a moment of pure receptivity. Defining a concept involves intentional action; so does resolving a contradiction into its ground. Yet the basic logical implications simply happen. Because they seldom occur in a pure form they are overlooked, yet they are the presuppositions that warrant all other associations. They establish the principles which our empirical streams of consciousness instantiate.

This dialectical moment of pure thought is the discovery that transformed logic for Hegel. And it was not a discovery by construction, but a discovery by careful, disciplined observation—by self-reflection. The self observed was not the idiosyncratic self of an early nineteenth-century Schwabian, but the self of a whole culture, the self of humankind. Therefore the validity of the discovery can be checked by others who perform the same disciplined observation.

Pure receptivity is the prerogative of the empiricists. They vaunt themselves on their submission to data—to the givens of experience. Yet here Hegel has discovered at the center of rational thought something simply given—a movement that simply happens. And that movement to something different generates the contradictions that lead to comprehensive truth. At the level of logic, at least, rationalism and empiricism are not contradictory opposites, but as activity and receptivity they are complementary components of a single complex development.

What do we say, however, when we turn to nature and history?

The world already is a continuum of space and time. And it offers a multitude of entities for observation. Can reason, by generating contradictions, infer the content of this multitude? Does Hegel have the resources to prove philosophically the existence of Herr Krug's pen?[3]

We already know enough to suspect that it is not that simple. Even the dialectical transitions of logic happen; they are not evident in their antecedents. When reason turns to the world, then, it cannot anticipate what will result from natural and historical processes. Any consequences will be givens to be noted empirically.

To be sure, logic can teach the observer that the results will be other, different, effected by causes and contingent. But it cannot flesh out these schematic characteristics with specific descriptions. Even in the philosophy of nature, Hegel cannot go where he pleases.

Yet reason is not left behind. For empiricism does not simply absorb a plethora of things and events. By paying attention to specific individuals, or rather classes of individuals, it determines the starting point for its investigations: colors, planets, acids, orchids, mammals, art, nation states.

It is a matter of pure contingency where one begins. One person becomes a botanist, a second an art historian. But their choices do not simply reflect what is given. They are brought to the data by the investigator.

However, Hegel does not simply collect the results of the various sciences. His *Encyclopedia* is not ordered according to some arbitrary or external standard, such as alphabetic sequence or year of occurrence. It is a system that moves progressively from logic to nature to man and society, from mechanics to physics to biology, from abstract right to morality to the social ethos. The contingency of arbitrary selection has been dissolved into the necessity of systematic development. Does this prejudice his empiricism?

To be sure, he does not create categories out of nothing. He runs through the gamut of the sciences of his time, both natural and human. And in his lectures, if not in his text, he shows himself conversant with the results of contemporary investigation.

The critical question concerns how the results of one science lead to the presuppositions of the next. For presuppositions there are—as we have seen. Investigators identify their data as bodies in motion or organisms, as minds or moral agents. Certainly transitions, processes, and developments occur in the world, generating change. Yet empirical researchers notice only those processes that are logically related to their starting point. The differences produced are of the same order, effects appropriate to the cause or properties appropriate to the subject matter. Such results do not lead of themselves to the preconceptions of a different discipline.

This is the point where Hegel introduces rationalism into the study of nature and history. Contradictions occur once starting point and result are considered together within a single rational perspective. When concepts are separated by time or focus the opposition is not noticed. Few empirical researchers consider the full complex of their investigations as a whole: starting points, processes, and results, not simply in terms of individuals, but in terms of kinds and classes, sorts and types. Hegel suggests that such a comprehensive review shows inherent contradictions in the diversity: an independence that is nonetheless essentially connected; a set of processes, each one leading to something different, yet as a whole returning to the point of departure.

Reason cancels the dispersion of space and time and identifies classes. The result is conceptual contradictions that push for resolution. It is Hegel's thesis that the concept that resolves the contradictions at one level becomes the starting point for empirical investigations at the next.

In other words, rationalism, with its interest in contradictions, provides the systematic connections between the empirical disciplines, justifying the different conceptual starting points. But it does not do so deductively. At each stage it is prey to the actual investigations undertaken by mechanics or chemistry, by psychology or sociology, by the history of nations and the history of religion. Once again rationalism and empiricism are not contradictories, but components of a single complex of intellectual disciplines.

Conceptual thought and the world of nature and history thus share the same form. There are discrete entities and there are processes or transitions from one thing to another. For all the difference in content, this isomorphism enables reason to apprehend things and events in time and space. It can recognize the structural similarity while taking note of the way in which external relations and contingencies differentiate nature and history into an alien reality.

We have, then, an Aristotelian motif in Hegel's theory. We know an alien matter because of an identity of form. But there is an important Kantian theme as well. For it is this identity of form that satisfies Kant's problem in the schematism: What makes it possible to apply concepts to the givens of experience in a way that does not misrepresent the world? Hegel answers by showing that nature and society instantiate logical concepts and logical transitions even as they introduce contingent and external variations. The identity makes it possible for reason to notice the differences, and apprehend the world as it really is.

But the identity does more. For reason takes the transitions in thought and experience, considers them together with their starting points in a single synthesis and, discovering a contradiction, speculatively articulates its ground or explanation. This is the genuinely creative move of rational thought. This it brings to its study of both nature and history. For Hegel, writing before Darwin had made the theory of evolution respectable, nature exemplified this increasing complexity not in terms of a temporal development, but in terms of an Aristotelian heirarchy of natural orders: mechanical, physical, organic, anthropological, social, and universal. In human history, however, rational consciousness is itself part of the reality being explained. It embodies implicitly the ongoing dynamic of reason: precise conceptual definition, reactions leading to unpredictable otherness, and comprehensive integrations of contradictory tensions. Reason, as Hegel himself says, is the philosophical name for Providence.

So ultimately Hegel is a rationalist. But reason is not simply conceptual definition, generalization, and the aversion to contradiction. It is also transitions that simply happen. To know itself it must be receptive. And that receptivity opens it empirically not only to itself but also to the world. Hegel is both a rationalist and an empiricist!

VIII

Concept and Time in Hegel

To formulate a philosophy of time is not easy, even though it would seem to be a basic requirement for any philosophy that attempts to comprehend the world of nature and history. The problem is briefly posed: Can the conceptual framework of philosophical thought do justice to the dynamic character of time?

The purpose of this chapter is not to provide a definitive answer to this question. Its aim is more limited. By discussing carefully the way in which Hegel's philosophy related conceptual thought to time, it hopes to provide new perspectives on this vexing philosophical problem.

I

Alexander Kojève's thesis in *Introduction to the Reading of Hegel* provides a good place to begin. He claims that Hegel identifies 'time' and 'concept'.[1] To justify this he refers to a statement made in Chapter VIII of the *Phenomenology* where Hegel writes: "*Time* is the *Concept* itself, which *exists*."[2] But when we check the passage, such a simple identification of concept and time is not obvious. Pausing only for a comma, Hegel goes on to write: "and as empty intuition [time] is presented to consciousness; therefore Spirit appears necessarily in time, and it appears in time as long as it does not *comprehend* its pure concept, that is, [as long as] it does not annul time."[3] If time is in consciousness only as empty *intuition*, it can hardly be identified with conceptual thought. And if the spirit is in time *only as long as* it has not comprehended its *concept*, the inescapable conclusion would be that the comprehended concept is quite distinct from the temporal process. The identity is not as simple as Kojève suggests.

79

But this leaves us with a basic question. What *is* the relation between time and concept for Hegel? Certainly he is not a Platonist, distinguishing the eternal real world, conceivable in itself, from the temporal phenomenal world of our representation and imagination. There is in Hegel an intrinsic relation between concept and time. In both his *Philosophy of History* and his *Phenomenology of Spirit*, he conceptually reconstructs developmental patterns in history.

A conceptual comprehension of history, however, cannot take place if the concept is time. Consider the following dilemma which results from such an identification: either the identity occurs at occasional moments of time, or it occurs in all of time. If we opt for the former alternative we land, as Kojève realizes, in scepticism. "Being *temporal*, the concept *essentially* changes; that is to say, there is no *definitive* knowledge, hence no *true* knowledge in the proper sense of the word."[4] But the other option is equally impossible. For the philosopher is himself a person in time. Either he must annul time in order conceptually to comprehend it (in which case the identity of time and concept breaks down), or his comprehension itself is but a moment in time which, again, makes it temporal. Kojève seems to opt for this alternative, but it lands him in a strange paradox, for the identity of time and concept is comprehended in the *last* moment of time which is no longer a temporal moment. "It is Eternity *engendered* by Time."[5] But what does this do for his simple identity as the principle of interpretation? If by concept we mean the content of philosophical thought, it seems rather inappropriate to say simply that "Time *is* the Concept."

While the conceptual comprehension of history cannot take place if time and concept are identical, neither can it take place if they are not related at all. If the concept is fundamentally nontemporal, it is incapable of incorporating without distortion that which is temporal and changing. For by transforming the dynamic of time into the static framework of thought, the unique characteristic of time is thereby destroyed, and there is no real *comprehension* at all.

Hegel recognized this dilemma and he attempted to face it directly. While he cannot simply identify time and concept as Kojève does, he must maintain that they are related—that time is the concept as it *exists*, that time is the concept as it is intuited rather than comprehended, and that there is a relation even though there is a fundamental difference.

This chapter explores how Hegel met this challenge. While acknowledging the importance of the *Phenomenology*, it reconstructs the argument from Hegel's *Encyclopedia*. It is my conviction that such an approach will throw light on the *Phenomenology* as a whole, as well as on the cryptic comment in Chapter VIII upon which Kojève based his interpretation.

II

We begin with Hegel's own discussion of time. Far from being ana-lyzed in the *Logic* (which is the realm of pure concepts), time is dis-cussed in the first chapter of the *Philosophy of Nature*.[6] In Paragraph 258 of the *Encyclopedia* Hegel writes: "Time, as the negative unity of externalized being, is at the same time something absolutely abstract, ideal. It is that being which, insofar as it *is*, is *not*, and insofar as it is *not, is;* the *intuited* becoming...."

Since this statement comes from the *philosophy* of nature, it is already an effort to conceptualize time. Yet it does seem to do justice to the temporal process itself.

Time has a dialectical character; that is, it becomes the opposite of what it was. The past, which was, is no longer; the future, which will be, is not yet. Only the present is, but it immediately ceases to be; and what now is not, comes into being. If we were to use the traditional language of philosophy to apply to this, we would say that in time 'being' becomes 'non-being,' while 'non-being' becomes 'being'. The first movement is from present to past; the second is from future to present.

With the introduction of ontological terms we become uncomfort-able. Almost intuitively we sense that such abstract terms are inap-propriate to the actual dynamic of the temporal process—that time *cannot* be comprehended in thought. Yet we can recognize that what we mean by 'time' is described by Hegel's statement: "It is that being which, insofar as it is, is not; and insofar as it is not, is." Within the being of time, there is movement from being to non-being, and from non-being to being. It is this *movement* which makes us uncomfortable with the abstract formulation that uses static terms like 'being' and 'non-being', and it is this movement which seems to resist conceptual comprehension.

From this preliminary look at Hegel's statement about the nature of time, the question is raised of how adequate conceptual thought is for expressing the movement of the temporal process. What, then, does Hegel mean when he uses the other term of our problem: 'concept'?

Hegel has already provided some direction in answering this ques-tion when he referred to time as "intuited *becoming*." Far from being discussed by Hegel in his philosophy of nature, the term 'becoming' is handled in the first chapter of his *Logic*. There he comes to it from the concepts 'being' and 'nothing'. These terms suggest a direct correspon-dence with the structure of time already discussed. If the correspon-dence holds, we will have achieved some measure of success in discov-ering the relation between time and concept in Hegel.

Before looking at the structure of conceptual thought as Hegel sees it, several comments are in order. In the first place, when talking about time we had to maintain the distinction between the temporal process itself and conceptual statements about it. So here we need to distinguish the process of thought, in its pure act of thinking concepts, from sense impressions and imagination which are set within a temporal and spatial context. We are concerned with the former: thought in its purest form, when it thinks the *meanings* of the terms involved apart from all mental images.

In the second place, we must allow thought to move, without trying to hold it artificially abstracted from the actual effort to think. In pure thought there is no distinction between the concept thought and the act of thinking. Therefore, when we think a concept and thought moves to thinking a related concept, that movement itself forms an aspect of thought. These two presuppositions are essential to understanding the nature of Hegel's *Logic*.[7]

Hegel begins by calling on thought to think the concept 'pure being'. This term represents what is thought when one endeavors to abstract from all specific determinations—that which is *common* to all things that are, in isolation from those characteristics that separate them. This concept of pure being is the most elementary concept in logic because it has no specific determinations at all. Its meaning is "that which is prior to all determination."

When thought thinks this concept, however, it discovers that it is thinking no thing. Since there are no determinations, there is nothing to be thought. There is no characteristic which can be the object of reflection. Thus, in the effort to think pure being, thought has moved, with a kind of inevitability, to thinking the concept 'nothing'.

As a second stage, thought now turns to this new concept nothing. It also has no determinations with which it can be thought. But in being that which has no character, it is the same as what thought had originally been thinking: the concept 'being'.

In the effort to think the concept of 'being', pure thought has found that it has moved in a circle. When it thought 'being' it moved to thinking 'nothing' and when it thought 'nothing' it moved to thinking 'being'. At this point, thought may take a significant step. Until now it has moved dialectically—an opposition between two concepts has developed within the seemingly inevitable movement of the thinking process itself. Hegel suggests that reason can think not only dialectically but also speculatively. That means, it can think the whole double movement as a unity. This unity involves both the movement from being to nothing and that from nothing to being. This new unified thought which encompasses the total movement through which we have gone introduces us to a new concept, 'becoming'. For becoming is the movement out of being into nothing and out of nothing into being.

The Hegelian concept of 'becoming' thus involves three distinct steps. In the first place there is the movement from 'being' to 'nothing'; in the second, the movement from 'nothing' to 'being'; and in the third, the essential unity of the two movements.[8]

The most elementary stage of conceptual thought for Hegel is this rational comprehension of the process of becoming. So this process becomes basic to all subsequent conceptual thought. For Hegel, the concept is intrinsically the *process* of becoming, by which 'being' becomes 'nothing' and 'nothing' becomes 'being'. If we substitute for the absolute term 'nothing' (or 'no thing') the relative term 'non-being', we can say that the logical concept 'becoming' grasps within rational, speculative thought that *movement* from being to non-being and from non-being to being which had appeared to be the nonconceivable residue in the structure of time.

Indeed, Hegel explicitly draws this relation when he says that time is "intuited becoming." And he goes on to add that it is not *in* time that everything arises and passes away, but that "time itself is this becoming, this arising and passing away."[9] We seem, then, to have reached the point where Kojève's identification of concept and time has been justified.

The identity, however, is not complete. Why does Hegel place his discussion of becoming at the beginning of the *Logic* as its first and most fundamental movement, while the discussion of time occurs in the philosophy of nature? Is he simply identifying logic with the philosophy of nature? But why, then, does he use the adjective "intuited"? For time is not a logical concept (else it would have been included as one moment of the *Logic*). It is rather a characteristic of existing reality—that reality which the philosophy of nature comprehends as *external* to thought. Time is not the product of thought's own activity in the sense that the concept 'becoming' is. It is intuited as already present in the world.

Closer inspection reveals more significant differences. The movement of conceptual thought began from, and returned to, being. But this is not true of time. The being of the present came from the non-being of the future and goes to the non-being of the past. It is being, not non-being, which is the middle term of the process, for the temporal process moves *from* non-being *through* being *to* non-being. This difference is significant, for it shows that, while time has the structure of 'becoming', it has inverted the content of that structure. The temporal process begins from non-being, while the conceptual process begins from being.

This leads to the second major difference. The triumph of the speculative move, for Hegel, was the recognition of the circularity of thought's movement: that the 'being' with which the process ended is the same as the 'being' with which it began. But this circularity cannot be claimed for time. The non-being of the future that will become the being of the present is not the same as the non-being of the past that the present has become. While the being is the present—the now—the two non-beings are not identical but fundamentally different. For the non-being of the past cannot become present in the way the non-being of the future can. This means that the inversion of the structure of becoming in time removes its circular character. Time is intuited as linear—an irreversible movement from future through present to past.[10]

We have, then, found a fundamental difference between conceptual thought and temporal process. Even though there is implicit in time the same basic structure as in the logic of becoming, the inversion of its content results in a linear rather than a circular movement.

To say, however, that time is the inverted form of 'becoming' is already an achievement. For it throws some light on a vexing problem in Hegel interpretation: the relation between the 'absolute idea' as the culmination of pure thought, and that nature which is the object of the philosophy of nature. In the *Encyclopedia*, Paragraph 247, Hegel says that nature "has come into being as the idea in the form of otherness." While that statement is difficult to explicate completely, we can at least recognize the otherness by which the logic of becoming (which is a component of the idea) is related to the temporal process (which is the condition of all natural existence). The otherness can be expressed as the inversion of content, while the relation is established through the similarity of structure.

The character of this 'otherness' illuminates the dialectical relation between philosophy and nature.[11] On the one hand, since time has the same structure as the logic of becoming, the implicit speculative character of the natural process is indicated. Conceptual thought can comprehend nature because both embody the process of becoming. On the other hand, even though time has the same structure, the content of this structure has been inverted, and as a result the circular character has been lost. This explains why the speculative character of nature is only implicit, and why the philosophy of nature does not pretend to reconstruct all that nature is. It can show that nature *has* this inverted character, but that which is *different* in the inverted character is not capable of being reproduced in the conceptual reconstruction. It is the contingent which cannot be expressed.

We have not resolved the dilemma, however, for it could be argued that, in comprehending temporal existence, speculative philosophy with its circular structure is distorting the linear movement of the natural process. If time is fundamentally linear, and if the speculative logic embodies a pattern of circles, then it would seem that the structural similarity is more apparent than real, and the differences are sufficiently significant to render the resolution precarious, if not futile. Far from there being an identity of concept and time, they seem to be so distinct that they are not capable of being related at all.

This conclusion is not drawn by Hegel. To say that time is the inverted form of becoming is only meaningful if it is possible, in some way, to *revert* the inversion. This suggests that one can annul the character of otherness so that the truth of time's content can be conceptually known. Indeed, Hegel suggests this when, in the *Phenomenology*, he equates "comprehending the pure concept" to "annulling time,"[12] and suggests that spirit is able to do both. Our next task, then, is to discover the steps by which Hegel reverts the inverted character of time so that its negative relation to the concept 'becoming' is itself negated, and the fundamental congruence of the two is established.

III

Within nature, the movement of time is never able to become articulated (even implicitly) as the process from non-being to being and back to non-being. All that *is* in nature is the present, with its changing content. There *is* neither past nor future; both are lost in void. The distinction between the three facets of time becomes a present reality only at the point where there is a kind of present which *relates to* past and future *as* nonexistent. The conscious subject establishes and maintains the difference through its memory and through its expectation.[13]

We move, then, beyond nature to spirit—to human, conscious life. The necessary condition for human consciousness is that it appear within a being which has natural existence. Hence it is located *in* space and time. But at the same time consciousness is able to view nature as a whole. In having the world as its object, it distinguishes itself from that world. This negative relation of otherness to the world enables spirit to rise above the immediate temporal condition and to view both past and future as moments within its present consciousness. This capacity of conscious spirit is the basic condition for ultimately reverting time's inverted character. But it is only the first, most primordial step.

Conscious spirit is temporal, even though it transcends its immediate present. There is a dialectical tension between its own location in time and its effort to rise above (or annul) time. If spirit can resolve this tension so that its own temporal character is overcome, it will complete the *re*version. The philosophy of spirit traces the development of this resolution in spirit's life.

We have noted that time's movement is from non-being to being and back to non-being. This movement can be annulled in two ways. On the one hand the non-being of past and future can be disregarded by focusing on the immediate consciousness of the present. This option, taken by romantics in both Hegel's time and ours, cannot be maintained, since the very effort to point out this present to consciousness is frustrated by the temporal movement of that present into the past.[14]

On the other hand, the character of past and future can be taken seriously, and thereby their 'non-being' reconstituted in the present's 'being' through the activity of conscious spirit. In this second process of transcending time, it is that negative determination of 'otherness' in past and future which is annulled, not its positive content.

This provides an important clue for resolving the relationship between concept and time. For we have seen that the conceptual process is circular: from being to non-being and back to being. If the linear movement of time can be so converted by spirit's activity that the non-being of the past is reconstituted in the being of the present, and the non-being of the future is projected from the being of the present, then, by thus "overreaching"[15] past and future, present spirit may revert the inverted character of time. On the one hand, the movement will be from the being of the present through the non-being of the past to the being of the present as memory; on the other hand, the being of the present through expectation will move to the non-being of the future which will in turn become the being of the present. In this way the linear character of time may be transformed into two circles that embody the logical structure of becoming. These two processes by which past and future are transcended in the present life of spirit constitute a fundamental theme of the philosophy of subjective and objective spirit.

In contrast to nature, spirit retains its past in its present through memory. Spirit recalls an intuition which had disappeared from consciousness. The non-being of the past can be called back into being, dissociated from its original temporal and spatial context, and reconstituted in the subjective time of the remembering individual. This process of memory separates the content of the remembered image from its specific temporal location and gives it a potentially universal character: it can be recalled many times.[16]

But the past retains a temporally determined character not yet overcome. As part of the temporal process, it has been conditioned by what preceded it in time. In other words, the content that has been reconstituted has not been derived from the present, but from what was past when it was present. This leaves the past which is simply remembered in imaginative thought with a residual contingency. Something more is required if the non-being of the past is to be completely transcended. Hegel claims that spirit has the power to meet this extra demand through conceptual thought.

Pure thought thinks the meanings of terms quite apart from their specific location in time and space. As it does so, the inevitable movement of dialectical thought traces the relationships which hold between these concepts. Speculative thought in its turn comprehends the *necessity* of these relations as independent of the temporal process.[17]

When spirit thinks about the past, then, it can organize the remembered conceptual content in such a way that the necessary relations which determined it are made clear. In this way the *process* which determined the past content is also reconstituted in the present life of spirit as necessary and another aspect of the residual contingency is overcome.

Despite this, spirit is not able to annul fully the non-being of the past. For the present activity of the intellect is still conditioned by its own temporal framework and by the perspective which it brings to the content it is attempting to understand. It cannot say what is *the* essential meaning of the past, remembered event. For the being of the present is not that being which determined the past to be what it was. Therefore it is left with some basic questions. Has the selective function of memory centered on the significant events of the past or only on incidental aspects? Will the future unfold in such a way that what appears to be essential now will be downgraded while other strands emerge as necessary? The circle has not been finally completed, because the individual humans who recall the past and comprehend its meaning were not the beings who constituted the past in the first place, nor will they be the beings who reflect on those same events a hundred years hence. Since they are finite in terms of their own temporal location, they are not able to determine what is *the* correct interpretation of the past. In other words, they are still subject to the fluctuation of subjective opinion, lacking the confidence that they have fully reconstituted the past in the present.

If the non-being of the past is reconstituted in the present through the remembering and conceiving activity of the intellect, the non-being of the future is projected from the present by the will in its freedom. The movement here is different from the preceding, because of the different nature of the temporal process and its role in the reverting activity. With regard to the past, the first movement of the logical structure of becoming (from being to non-being) is present in the temporal process itself as the condition for the activity of spirit in reconstituting the past in the present as the second movement. Here, however, the temporal process embodies the second movement of becoming—from non-being to being. To complete the circle of becoming, the first movement must be established. From the being of the present there is to be an action or projection to the non-being of the future such that the temporal process becomes the return to being of that which has been projected from being.

In this movement we cannot presuppose the temporal process in order to transcend it. On the contrary, we must explain how the conscious spirit acts such that the temporal process fulfills its expectation.

Spirit anticipates the future with hope and fear. Acting with the intention that the hopes will be fulfilled and the fears proven groundless, spirit learns that it has the capacity to affect that future. The will, reacting to its anticipations, has changed the nature of that which was anticipated. Just as through memory spirit learned that it could reconstitute the past, so through action it learns that it can determine the future. As will becomes conscious of this capacity, it sets for itself goals to be achieved. It begins to initiate the first movement of the logic of becoming from being to non-being. The act of will in the present intends to so determine the future that when the future becomes present it will *be* what was intended.

Once again, however, spirit finds that its intentions are not fulfilled. Just as, in the previous discussion, memory was still bedevilled by the contingency of the content, so here spirit discovers that its intended future is not what actually comes to be. It does not have the power in the present so to project into the future that the future being will be exactly what it intended.

This failure of will to achieve its goal can be traced to the character of non-being that marks the future. For the future is not simply the future of isolated individuals, but of groups of people—indeed, of everybody. The actions of others also influence what will be. And the reflection by spirit on the nature of will leads it to realize that if it is to transcend time, it must so cooperate with other finite humans that together they are involved in the process of determining the future.

Just as, in the recollection of the past, conceptual thought was that which gave us the capacity to transcend the contingencies of memory, so the awareness of collective responsibility for the future gives us the capacity to transcend the limitations of our own individual wills. There can develop cooperation between individual and social will, such that common action does not destroy the freedom of the individual and the individual does not do violence to general will.

Again, however, this analysis does not solve our dilemma. How ought we to act? What should the relationships between individuals be? What should each individual contribute to the actual decisions of political processes and the course of historical events? Once again we need a standard to determine what is significant and what is not. Individuals within a state do not necessarily know what is of value to the state or to humanity generally. There are unforeseen circumstances, and the significance of certain kinds of actions is not known. What is ultimately of importance in the process by which men and women, through their wills, determine the future?

If the circle of the past had been completed, the solution here might have been easier. For the past is the process by which we have become what we are. If we could have an unambiguous interpretation of the past, so that we knew what we were, then we would know the nature of the self which was determining the future. If we could comprehend what was essential and what was inessential in nature and history we would have a frame of reference for our action with regard to the future. But as we have seen, this has not been achieved.

Even if it could be achieved, it would not help. For the individuals who act are but a part of the whole. Their actions must fit in with the actions of all others if they are to achieve their goals. But as individuals they do not know what other people are deciding at this very moment, whether they are acting on the basis of reason or on subjective desire, and how those actions will determine the future. Since the actions of others will affect the success of any projections into the future, people can neither foretell the future, nor say with finality what any individual or society ought to do, even if they be the wisest of governors.[18]

We have again arrived at an impasse. We find that the effort to transcend the future is blocked by human finitude. There is always that in the future which is not determined by what we consciously will to happen. There is the influence of subconscious and unconscious motives, the influence of desires hidden and unnoticed. And hence there is a quality of indeterminateness about the future which has not been annulled. In addition, the being of the future, which is being determined by this present act, may come to be at a time when the one who acts is no longer, so that there is once again a lack of identity between the initiating and the concluding 'being'. The effort to establish a full circle between present being and future being has not been successful.

Our analysis of both memory and expectation has posed us with problems. Each of these activities was not able to achieve its goal of reverting the temporal process because each began from a present being that was able neither to reconstitute what was essential in the past, nor to anticipate what would be significant in the future. The present being of the philosopher or of the political agent is itself temporal and finite. They can only hope to annul time fully if they can relate themselves to that which is ultimate and infinite—to that *present* being which has determined the past to be what it was, and which will determine the future to be what it will be. This infinite reality, eternally present, is what religion seeks to know. The ultimate achievement of reverting the inverted form of time can only take place *if* we can come to know unambiguously the nature of ultimate reality such that we can recognize what is essential in the past as the consequent of that present reality, and feel confident that what will be significant in the future is already implicit in that present. If we are to complete our examination of the relation between concept and time in Hegel, we must turn to what he says about religion.

IV

Our problem has developed to its critical point. The structural relation between time and conceptual thought can be finally established only *if* present being constitutes both the past and the future in their non-being. But finite humans on their own cannot effect this constituting activity. They approximate it through memory and conceptual thought on the one hand, and through will and conscious collective responsibility on the other. But approximation is not enough. The structure of 'becoming' is circular because it begins and ends from the same point: the concept of 'being'. But man's being is finite and discrete, whether as an individual or in society. And this finitude cannot transcend its limits simply by asserting its identity with that Being which determined the past and which will determine the future. For that assertion itself is radically conditioned by finitude. Indeed, because our reason and will are finite, we cannot on our own grasp what is ultimately significant about past or future, and therefore cannot reconstruct the circle even *conceptually*.

There are here two options which we must distinguish. On the one hand, through religion, we become *identified in being* with the absolute so that it is our own, now infinite, being that has determined past and future. On the other, we come to the realization that we share the life of the absolute while yet remaining specifically located both spatially and temporally. The shared life enables us to comprehend what is significant in past and future—to comprehend that past and future have been and will be determined by this ever-present life—without thereby giving us the authority to claim that we, continuing as finite individuals, determine the being of past and future. In this second alternative, we do not escape time through religion, but we are made fully aware of the eternal dimension of time through the complete disclosure of infinite life.

If we were to characterize these two alternatives in religious terms, we would refer to Hinduism and Christianity. The ultimate insight of the former is that *atman* is *Brahman*—that the being of the individual spirit is ultimate reality. In contrast, the latter asserts, not that humans *become* God, but that they will share in the life of God as children, and that the spiritual presence of this life will teach us "all things" (John 14:26). Indeed the believer goes so far as to say that "it is no longer I who live, but Christ lives in me; and the life I now live in the flesh I live by faith in the Son of God" (Galatians 2:20).

Even a brief consideration of the Hegelian corpus leaves no doubt concerning the option Hegel has taken. The penultimate chapter of the *Phenomenology* (as of the *Encyclopedia*) is entitled "Revealed Religion,"[19] and is followed only by a discussion of absolute knowing or philosophy. And while there were variations of order in the *Lectures on the Philosophy of Religion*, invariably Hegel ended with his discussion of Christianity.

But if Hegel opts for Christianity as the religious means by which we transcend our finitude, he is faced with a problem. We have seen that the only way in which time can be *re*verted is by reconstituting the past in, and projecting the future from, the present. In addition we have argued that memory and thought on the one hand cannot of themselves ensure that they have *the* correct conceptual comprehension of the past, and that will and collective ethical activity on the other cannot of themselves fully determine in the present what will be in the future, because they can never know what will be significant in the future. If we were infinite reality in simple identity, then, when we probe beneath the surface of things we will become immediately aware of the truth of past and future as the truth of our own being, because our being has thereby annulled its finitude. But if we retain our finitude as a necessary condition of our being even as we share in infinite life, then the possibility of ambiguity remains. For we cannot *know* whether our part of the infinite Life is that which is essential or not.

This problem would condemn to failure Hegel's attempt to *re*vert time, unless he can show that Christianity is able to ensure an unambiguous perspective for the finite individual. He asserts that it does. There are three aspects to this assertion.

In the first place, Christianity claims that the temporal order, with its finite individuals, was created by the eternal Infinite. This Infinite then became a finite individual in time, thereby revealing that the temporal order was not alien from itself. When this man, Jesus of Nazareth, encountered the radical limits of his finitude in death, he was raised into the infinite, universal life of spirit. The present being of the Infinite, then, as revealed in this report, is not alien to finitude, but rather incorporates the finite as a necessary moment of its life.

In the second place, Hegel refers to the Lutheran proclamation of justification not by works but by faith. This affirmation conjoins the despair of ever achieving salvation through one's finite action and effort with the discovery of infinite life through believing acceptance of the report of Jesus' death and resurrection. Passing through despair in their own finitude, individuals experience the infinite life of spirit.

This leads, in the third place, to a recognition of the essential unity of the two movements. Both what is reported in Christian doctrine and what is experienced in believing existence embody the identical structure of finitude being incorporated into the infinite. This identity of structure enables believing individuals to *recognize* that they have within their own existence the pattern of infinite life. They escape the threat of ambiguity because infinite life, so experienced, is not opposed to finite life, but has finitude as an essential moment of itself. Even though they have not become identical in being with the infinite, believers can know unambiguously that they share the divine life of the spirit. On this basis they can interpret the past and anticipate the future without the threat of inevitable distortion from their remaining finitude.[20]

We must note explicitly the nature of the reversion achieved. Believers have recognized that their own present being shares in the infinite life of ultimate reality even though they have not become fully identified with it. Therefore they *recognize* conceptually that the reconstruction of the past and the anticipation of the future embody the circular structure of 'becoming'; but whenever they *act* in the present they cannot change the past, nor can they fully determine the future. While their thoughts can share in the life of the absolute, their practical actions cannot. Therefore their realization is twofold. On the one hand, they can recognize the truth of the past since the present life of spirit both constituted, and is constituted by, that past. But on the other, they act with no assurance at all that they are thereby generating what will be significant in the future, for spirit's present encompasses much more than their individuality.

Thus, political agents, even if they be "philosopher kings," cannot be confident about the results of their actions, even though they have faith in the ultimate providential direction of history. Philosophers, however, can unite the speculative power of reason with the knowledge that they share the life of absolute spirit. They have thereby the principle of interpretation which can recognize both the significance of history and how absolute knowledge has become possible for them. In their conceptual thought they have the power to *revert* time's *in*version, not by making the past present in reality, but by comprehending the present necessity of the past's development and history. Through faith and the insight derived therefrom, they have been able to "annul time" by "comprehending the pure concept." From this vantage point they can recognize that "time is the concept which exists (*der da ist*)."[21]

Thus Hegel is neither a Platonist, placing concepts and ideas in a timeless eternity, nor a pragmatist, reducing thought simply to a temporally conditioned and relative perspective. While he maintains a sharp distinction between concept and time, he yet maintains they are integrally related. To say, as Kojève does, that Hegel identifies concept and time is far too simple. It is only a part of the truth, and as part it distorts the intention of the Hegelian philosophy. In Hegel's view the identity can only be asserted because the difference has been taken seriously. For the keynote of his system is the "identity of identity and non-identity."[22] Cryptically, this statement expresses the results of our analysis of the relation between concept and time in Hegel's philosophy.

IX

The Inequity of Equality

Towards the end of his essay on the English Reform Bill, published in the last year of his life, Hegel had some strong words to say about the principle of equality, as it had found expression in French political life:

> Instead of that activity of institutions in which public order and genuine freedom consists, recourse was had once more to these generalities which, by what they demand in the way of freedom, make constitutional law self-contradictory from the start. Obedience to the law is granted to be necessary, but when demanded by the authorities, i.e., by individuals, it is seen to run counter to freedom. The right to command, the difference arising from this right, the general difference between commanding and obeying, is contrary to equality. A multitude of men can call itself a 'people', and rightly, because 'people' is just this indefinite multitude; but authorities and officials, in general the members of the organized power of the state, are different from the 'people', and they are therefore to be in the wrong; they have forsaken equality, and they stand over against the 'people' which has the infinite advantage of being recognized as the sovereign will. In the circle of this extreme contradiction a nation revolves once it has been dominated by these abstract categories.[1]

This condemnation of liberty and equality, if not of fraternity, is made by a person who, in his student days, celebrated the fall of the Bastille. Does it, then, represent the shift, frequently seen in our own day, from student radical to hide-bound reactionary—from the emotional enthusiasm of a naive belief in human goodness, to the equally

95

emotional disillusion with all moral principles? To use Popper's terms: is the mature Hegel an enemy of the open society?

When we turn to the body of Hegel's writings, we find that he did not come to his distrust of the principle of equality late in life. In the *System of Ethical Life*, a manuscript dating from 1802, just after his return to university for graduate studies, he talks about equality as holding between classes, or between estates, but not between individuals. "Equality is nothing but an abstraction—it is the formal thought of life...and this thought is purely ideal and without reality. In reality, on the other hand, it is the inequality of life which is established, and therefore the relation [of lordship] and bondage."[2]

This early comment is developed further in the *Phenomenology*. In this work, Hegel is not focusing particularly on political questions. It represents his counterpart for epistemology; the discussion of equality emerges at the stage where a society, confident in its own achievements, claims to know the truth about the social order. This happens in the Roman empire, where citizens are equals as persons. *Person*, here, is used not in our modern way—as a sexless substitute for man—but in the legal sense of having status before the law. The equality of persons entails an equal right to hold property. But this equality of right does not carry with it an equality of fact. Not only is there a great disparity in actual property—a disparity generated by the inequality of capacity, but there is as well a concentration of power in the hands of one man, the emperor.[3]

Equality becomes a political principle only because those claiming to know the truth about society abstract a particular feature of human existence, ascribe to it essential significance, and then disregard the other features which provide the conditions for, have resulted from, or disturb the equilibrium of, the features so isolated.

'Equality', then, is of necessity an equality of right and not of fact. For facts are complex, influenced by and influencing their context and setting. As such, strict identity can seldom be established. In their distinctive singularity they are diverse. Any equality to be ascribed to them in truth cannot be an equality empirically discovered, but one which is imputed through an intellectual process that ignores diversity and postulates a similarity. Under Roman law, this similarity is the similarity of right, the right to hold property, and hence the right to be recognized as an independent agent.

When the 'ought' of right becomes a political principle that is not only to be acknowledged as valid, but also implemented in fact, we have moved from Roman society to the French Revolution. Hegel does not mention equality in his discussion of this stage of social development; he is more interested in the principle of freedom. Nevertheless, it is equality which provides the motor for the inherent development. Equality is to be established in the political order. Some people undertake to establish it. But in undertaking that task they inevitably assume a right to command and order social life which distinguishes them from those commanded and ordered. In principle when they command, they are merely implementing political principles. In fact, however, their commands reflect their particular judgements, which in turn reflect their specific personality—that which distinguishes them from their fellows. This, then, produces the contradiction to which Hegel referred in his essay on the English Reform Bill. It is a contradiction between principle and fact. Both are supposed to embody equality in the same way and in the same respect; precisely on that account they come in conflict.[4]

The inadequacy of equality as a political principle is reaffirmed in the manuals Hegel published for his lecture courses. In the *Encyclopedia* he adds a remark to Paragraph 539 that stresses the abstract nature of the principle of equality.

> The familiar proposition, All men are by nature equal, blunders by confusing the 'natural' with the 'concept'. It ought rather to read: *By nature* men are only unequal. But the *concept* of liberty, as it exists as such, without further specification, is abstract subjectivity, as a person capable of property.... But that this freedom should exist, that it should be *man* that is recognized and legally regarded as person, is so little *by nature*, that it is rather only a result and product of the consciousness of the deepest principle of mind, and of the universality and expansion of this consciousness.

Similarly, to paragraph 200 of the *Philosophy of Right* Hegel adds the remark:

> Men are made unequal by nature, where inequality is in its element, and in civil society the right of particularity is so far from annulling this natural inequality that it produces it out of mind and raises it to an inequality of skill and resources, and even to one of moral and intellectual attainment. To oppose to this right a demand for equality is a folly of the understanding, which takes as real and rational its abstract equality and its 'ought-to-be'.

In these two quotations Hegel argues that equality is not a characteristic of man, not even a natural right, but that it is rather the product of intellectual reflection. It is a *concept*, the product of the *under-standing*. To get to the roots of his characterization of equality, then, we turn to his discussion of the concept of equality in the *Logic*. For the *Logic* is where Hegel outlines the way in which the intellect reasons.

The term 'equality' emerges in Hegel's discussion of the concept 'diversity'. 'Diversity' is not an original concept. The intellect comes to this notion from its reflection on the concept of difference. Pure difference, in isolation from all other notions, cannot be consistently thought. For difference could then only be different from difference. The very effort to think this thought makes reflection aware that difference is a relative term, not an independent one. 'Difference' is the correlative of 'identity'. When thought differentiates it presupposes a context, single and continuous, into which differences are introduced.

While identity and difference are correlatives, though, they need not be applied to something in the same respect. What can be identified in one way may be differentiated in another. It is this complex of an identity which is indifferent to a difference, and vice versa, which is meant by the term 'diversity'.

Diversity, then, involves both some kind of identity and some kind of difference, as well as the indifference of the one to the other. What one identifies does not tell us what is to be differentiated, nor does the reverse occur. The identification is not inherent in the subject matter of the analysis, but is introduced by reflection. In other words, reflective thought takes its diverse subject matter and identifies in it a likeness—an equality. But this leaves as its counterpart a residue of unlikeness or inequality.[5] The two are contrasted by reflective thought, but are not inherent in the original diversity. Equality and inequality are external to that subject matter, and a product of external reflection. For reflection has simply paid attention to features it finds similar and ignored dissimilarity. The similarity is not a constituent feature that demands to be acknowledged.[6]

This analysis of the concept 'equality' claims that it is an abstraction, introduced by a thinking process which is independent of, and indifferent to, its subject matter. It is simply the interest of reflection that identifies 'equality'. As such, equality is the result of understanding; it is an abstract notion, not something natural or inherent.

Does this claim land Hegel in the camp of the reactionaries—those who rejected the liberal reforms of the French Revolution and the early nineteenth century in Germany, France, and England? I do not think so. And I take this position not simply because Hegel went to Berlin in 1817 as a part of the liberal leadership of the Prussian regime.[7] I want to suggest that Hegel's criticism of 'equality' is part of a conceptual analysis of thought and political life that probes deeper than superficial radical or reactionary ideology.

As a first step in developing this suggestion, let us return to Hegel's logic. We have seen that equality is indifferent to whatever is dissimilar. But both are the product of external reflection. That reflection can decide to think equality together with the inequality—to oppose the one to the other. This synthesis, or the thinking of them together, is not entirely arbitrary; after all, both terms were abstractions from the same subject matter. The synthesis represents an effort to get back to a more adequate understanding of what is going on. The only trouble is that we end up with opposites being referred to the same thing: a contradiction. And a contradiction cannot really be thought in a single complex thought. It collapses.

Yet, while external reflection abstracted the equality and the inequality, it did not simply create them out of whole cloth. There must be something in the original subject matter that suggested the similarity and the dissimilarity. Therefore the contradiction is not simply an aberration of confused thought; there is something behind it—a reason or ground. So the intellect needs to find the ground out of which equality and inequality arise. And that ground will indicate how the subject matter is in fact characterized.[8]

Whatever ground we find, it will be a universal, just as 'equality' is a universal. But it will be a universal of a different sort. We have seen that 'equality' is an abstraction. External reflection pays attention to some similarity and ignores everything else. This similarity or likeness is common to a number of individuals because their distinctive differences are disregarded. But a ground or reason is different. Although also a universal, it will explain why the particular features are the way they are—how the similarities are generated and why the differences result. It performs the functions of an explanatory hypothesis, to use more modern parlance.

Let me illustrate. An abstract universal is like the concept 'red' which we have abstracted from a stop sign, a fire truck, and a Christmas candle. External reflection has identified the similarity among this diverse collection, while ignoring the differences. The other kind of universal (which we might call concrete in contrast with abstract) is like the term 'apple', which integrates and explains the roundness, the redness, the taste, the seeds, the blossoms and leaves on the tree from which it comes, and the pies into which it might go. All these different features, in their differences and with their contingent variations, are brought together into the single general concept 'apple'. When looked at in this way, 'apple' is a concrete universal (although from another perspective—as what is common to a MacIntosh, a Delicious, and a Russet—it, too, could be considered as an abstraction). The concrete universal is not simply a result of external reflection; it responds to the diverse features of a thing and explains them in terms of their ground or specific nature.

How does this logical point relate to the political questions with which we began? What does it mean when we want to talk about society in terms of concrete universals? I would like to take two steps in answering this question. The first will consider Hegel's model for social organization as outlined in the *Phenomenology*. The second will suggest how this model is to be applied in a political constitution.

Early in the *Phenomenology*, at the beginning of the section on lordship and bondage, Hegel discusses the concept of recognition. Just prior to this discussion he says that the concept of spirit is emerging, and spirit is the term he uses for the social order—the interaction of individuals—in which 'I' identify myself with 'we', and 'we' identify ourselves with 'I'. In other words, the concept of recognition provides the model that explains how a social unit can have a concrete identity; how it is not simply a collection of individuals but has its own singular character.

In characterizing the concept of recognition, Hegel considers the simplest structure: the encounter of two individuals. There are four stages to this encounter. At first, one notices that the other is like herself—that the two are similar. But she does not want to lose her individuality and uniqueness, so in the second place she reacts against this identification and affirms her difference from him. In the third place, however, she realizes that in the reaction she is just like him, because he is equally different from her. Therefore there is a dynamic relation in which she recognizes him as different from herself, even though that recognition is based on their similarity; and she acknowledges that he is similar in affirming his difference while she affirms hers.

This dynamic is only half the story, however. For on the fourth level of the analysis he experiences the same three stages in his encounter with her. In fact, his experience is part of the dynamic that produces her reaction, and vice versa. There is thus a play of forces in which the identity and the difference are in tension. Both acknowledge how they are similar yet also different, and that acknowledging involves a continual reaction, moving from identifying to differentiating and back again.[9]

This analysis of the concept of recognition is a model, sketched as occurring between two individuals. But Hegel suggests that it characterizes the social relation generally, where a number of individuals are involved in the play of forces. This much more complex interaction develops a distinctive character which is constituted by the differences of the many individuals as well as by their similarities—not only the similarities all share, but also the partial similarities that characterize segments of the society. The result is a concrete universal, for a correct theoretical description of that society will represent it in such a way that the individuals are not identified according to a few abstract features, but rather the description will show how their differences as well as their similarities interact to create the distinctive character of that society.

In this characterization of how society is constituted, Hegel has taken his distance from Rousseau. For Rousseau's general will abstracts from the particular wills of individuals in a society. Any expression of particularity is to be avoided. For Hegel, on the contrary, that particularity is precisely what has to be taken into account in understanding and explaining the social order. In fact, it generates the dynamic which constitutes that order, and any abstract similarity, any abstract equality, does not take account of the differences that constitute the members of the society as distinct individuals, nor does it integrate them into the society. It is thus fundamentally inequitable.

This conviction underlies Hegel's description of the political order. There are not simply individuals on the one hand and society at large on the other. Individuals interact according to their interests and needs, and this interaction produces social units that integrate sets of interests and needs. Hegel discusses these social units under the term 'corporation', This term probably referred to the incorporated communities of his time where a town, formed around a particular economic focus, had developed its distinctive character. The individuals participate in civic life in terms of both their common interests and their distinctive contributions and needs.[10]

His stress on these specific social structures has its implications for his constitutional proposals. A viable constitution, he suggests, will not involve a representation of individuals as individuals. Such a representative democracy would abstract from the specific differences and characteristics of its citizens and would consider them only as persons having a right to property or, as in the English Reform Bill, having a certain minimum property. This would result in a legislature that focused entirely on the interests of property to the exclusion of everything else.

Instead, representation should, in the first place, be divided between the agricultural class and the commercial class. These two classes will have their distinctive modes of contribution to the political order reflected in the traditional English division between Lords and Commons, or in the French division between the estates. The agricultural class can assume responsibility in the legislature by birth, because land is transferred from generation to generation. The commercial class, however, is not static; it fluctuates in response to economic conditions and needs. And it will be represented in the legislature most adequately through the concrete, limited corporations that have emerged in civil society. Each corporation has its distinctive character that incorporates the diversity of its membership. Its representative would bring that distinctness to the legislature, where the diversity of corporate interests would interact to produce a community in which the differences between them are taken as seriously as their shared interests. Within this representative structure of the legislature, the corporations would stand as equals of each other; that very equality would ensure that their differences—the way they are unequal—is taken into account.

When making the appointment of deputies to the legislature, Hegel writes,

> Society is not dispersed into atomic units, collected to perform only a single and temporary act, and kept together for a moment and no longer. On the contrary, it makes the appointment as a society, articulated into associations, communities, and corporations which, although constituted already for other purposes, acquires in this way a connection with politics.[11]

Such a legislature will in fact express the integrated character of a concrete social order.

We can now draw our moral. Equality is inequitable because it abstracts from the complexity of the social order by isolating in thought a particular idealized feature. Equity is achieved not by appealing to such abstract principles, but by taking seriously the associations and corporate structures that in fact emerge in society at large and having these contribute through their representatives to the legislative process.

CHRISTIANITY

X

'Unhappy Consciousness' in Hegel:
An Analysis of Medieval Catholicism?

Hegel's *Phenomenology of Mind* does not fit easily into the traditional categories of philosophical literature. On the one hand, it does not appear to be epistemology, outlining the universal conditions necessary for any knowledge at all, for it explores stages of development that fit into some historical periods and not others. On the other hand, it is not a philosophy of history, for it does not trace a linear historical sequence from stage to stage. The advanced achievements of understanding precede the elemental desires of the person who has virtually no self-consciousness, for example, and the discussion of primitive, totemistic religions follows the liberation of the enlightenment and the French Revolution.

This difficulty of categorization has presented a challenge to scholars. As they move from section to section in the *Phenomenology*, they have looked for the concrete historical situations to which Hegel refers. Or they have sought those analyses of the human condition which would make each stage a part of the universal structure of consciousness. The first tendency has been particularly strong with the section on unhappy consciousness. Enlightened moderns have disdained any thought that such practices as thoughtless devotion, ascetic self-denial, and the reliance on another to mediate truth could be a universal condition of personal development. Therefore they are taken to be descriptions of medieval Catholicism, a stage totally transcended and left behind.

The explanatory footnotes in this section of the first English translation point the reader in this direction. For example, the three forms of the unchangeable are said to be "God as Judge," "Christ," and

"The religious communion."[1] Elsewhere reference is made to "the historic Christ as worshipped, e.g. in the medieval church," the Crusades, asceticism, the priesthood, and the use of Latin in church services.[2] The unwary can be excused for imagining that these notes stem from the hand of Hegel himself, and that the original intention of the text was to refer explicitly to medieval Catholicism.

The footnotes, however, are not in the original German. Indeed, a first reading of the text would give no immediate occasion for supposing that it is describing Christian phenomena. The vocabulary includes terms like 'the changeable' and 'the unchangeable', or 'particularity' and 'individuality' contrasted with 'universality'. Such abstract philosophical terms do not indicate any specific historical referent for the discussion.

In his prefatory comment on the section, the English translator Baillie, expands on the point made in his footnotes: "The background of historical material for this type of mind is found in the religious life of the Middle Ages and the mental attitude assumed under the dominion of the Roman Catholic Church and the Feudal Hierarchy." Even though Baillie admits that "these are merely instances of an experience found in all mankind," he goes on to affirm that "Hegel selects forms assumed in European history, and has these in mind throughout the succeeding analysis."[3]

To what extent is Baillie's claim justified? Does this section of the *Phenomenology* analyze one particular epoch, or does it represent a universal characteristic of human nature?

To answer this question we need a criterion for distinguishing a unique historical period from an experience that is found more generally—what we shall call a "universal experience." Two related characteristics will serve. In the first place, a historical period is unique because it is, in some sense, unrepeatable. When it has become part of cultural memory it endures as a component within a more complex development, and as such cannot be recreated in its pristine innocence. In contrast, a universal experience is common to different periods and can be generalized by disregarding specific conditions.

In the second place, it is the total set of historical conditions which render one stage concrete and unrepeatable. Only in light of the complete context can that stage be understood logically. In contrast, a universal experience is abstract and can be examined in isolation. To be sure, each concrete setting will affect the way in which that experience appears. But the analysis is concerned, not with these specific (and in some sense accidental) factors, but with a structure that is logically independent of the various situations. It does not require concrete reference and can be expressed abstractly.

Our question has now been defined more precisely. Is the analysis of unhappy consciousness *abstracted* from particular settings, or does it require reference to concrete conditions to be logically complete? Alternatively, is the stage of unhappy consciousness repeatable, and in fact repeated, within the development of history, or is it simply a seldom-recalled moment within a cultural memory?

I

On first glance, the text itself seems to justify Baillie's suggestion that Hegel has "the forms assumed in European history...in mind." Unhappy consciousness develops from stoicism and scepticism and these movements were current in imperial Rome. Indeed Hegel uses the term 'stoicism' because that was what the freedom of consciousness was called when it "appeared as a phenomenon conscious of itself in the course of the history of man's spirit." In conscious allusion to both Marcus Aurelius and Epictetus he says that "the essence of this consciousness is to be free, on the throne as well as in fetters, throughout all the dependence that attaches to its individual existence...." He locates the phenomenon even more specifically within history when he writes: "It is a freedom which can come on the scene as a general form of the world's spirit only in a time of universal fear and bondage, a time, too, when mental cultivation is universal, and has elevated culture to the level of thought."[4] Much later, in his lectures on the history of philosophy, Hegel said that, along with Platonists, Aristotelians, and Epicureans, there can no longer be any stoics.[5]

This suggests that stoicism occurs only when a number of conditions are present. In addition to the "universal fear and bondage" of the slave, there is "universal mental cultivation" which "has elevated culture to the level of thought."[6] It appears that this concrete historical phenomenon can never be repeated in its original simplicity.

To reawaken [it] would be to try to bring back to an earlier stage the mind of a deeper culture and self-penetration.... It would be an impossibility and as great folly as were a man to wish to expend his energies in attaining the standpoint of youth, the youth in endeavouring to be the boy or child again.[7]

The phenomena analyzed in this section of the *Phenomenology* seem to be neither abstract nor repeatable.

Further evidence to support this interpretation can be found in Hegel's lectures on the *Encyclopedia*. While the small chapter entitled

"Phenomenology of Mind" in that schema does not pretend to encompass the broad scale of his earlier work, Hegel does discuss consciousness and self-consciousness, and in particular the life-and-death struggle and lordship and bondage.[8] The original text is brief and condensed. Of more direct interest to us are the comments made in Hegel's lectures which the editor has added as "Zusätze" or additions to the various sections.

When referring to the life and death struggle, Hegel says:

> To prevent any possible misunderstanding with regard to the standpoint just outlined, we must here remark that the fight for recognition pushed to the extreme here indicated *can only occur in the natural state*, where men exist only as single, separate individuals; but it is absent in civil society and the State because here the recognition for which the combatants fought already exists.[9]

This stage, Hegel affirms, is unrepeatable. While it may have been found under different conditions in different parts of the world in the early stages of human development, it is not an instance "of an experience that is strictly found in all mankind."[10]

His comments on lordship and bondage, however, point in a different direction. To be sure, the specific historical references are to Pisistratus in Athens and the strict rule of the kings in Rome. But his comments are more general: "This subjugation of the slave's egotism forms the *beginning* of true human freedom. This quaking of the single, isolated will, the feeling of the worthlessness of egotism, the habit of obedience, is a necessary moment in the education of all men."[11] The moment analyzed in "lordship and bondage" is abstract, independent of any particular historical context, and is, hence, explicitly repeatable.

This suggestion of the universal possibility of subjugation is supported when we look elsewhere in the *Phenomenology*. The religion of God as pure light "includes within it the form which we found in the case of immediate self-consciousness, the form of lord and master, in regard to the self-consciousness of spirit which retreats from its object."[12] Slave-consciousness, then, is not found simply as a secular response to a political power[13] or to the individual slave-owner but as a religious response to a transcendental Lord.

Baillie's footnote to the passage just quoted refers to Judaism and Muhammedanism. A phrase in the discussion of the slave seems to point in the same direction: "Albeit the fear of the Lord is the beginning of wisdom," Hegel writes, "consciousness is not therein aware of being self-existent."[14] The subordinate clause is an explicit quotation from Hebrew scriptures.[15] We should not be surprised, then, to discover that, in his *Lectures on the Philosophy of Religion*, Hegel develops the motif of slave-consciousness in his discussion of Judaism.[16]

The evidence suggests that the stage analyzed by Hegel as lordship and bondage can be abstracted from any one particular historical context. It is a facet of human experience to be found repeated under distinctly different conditions. Indeed Hegel has gone so far as to suggest in the *Encyclopedia* that anyone who has not had his egoistic will broken by the discipline of a fearful master cannot discover the genuine freedom of human maturity. This subjugation of the will must be experienced by each one personally; it cannot be simply relived as a moment of cultural memory.

Considerations so far seem to lead to contrary conclusions. On the one hand stoicism and the life-and-death struggle seem to be unrepeatable and unique. By analogy they would support Baillie's suggestion that medieval Christianity is the specific locus of unhappy consciousness. On the other hand, the results of our discussion of lordship and bondage lead to the inference that unhappy consciousness may be the analysis of a phenomenon abstracted from a number of distinct historical settings. Can we resolve this apparent dilemma through a second look at the section on stoicism?

That discussion does not include all facets of stoic theory. While it refers to the calm assurance of self-consciousness, which reduces the diversity of natural existence to the simplicity of a single thought, it ignores the whole area of stoic political philosophy. This is picked up explicitly later in the *Phenomenology* in the section "Legal Status": "What in Stoicism was implicit merely in an abstract way is now an explicit *concrete* world."[17] Is stoical self-consciousness but an abstracted moment of a concrete historical situation after all?

The introduction to Hegel's chapter "Spirit" provides an answer to that question. In this section Hegel considers spirit as a concrete historical totality, constituted by the interaction of individuals within a society. Only within the social context, where the individual contributes by thought and action to the well-being of others, and in turn benefits from their activity, does self-sufficiency become possible. Hegel writes:

> Spirit is...the self-supporting, absolutely real ultimate being. All the previous modes of consciousness are abstractions from it: they are constituted by the fact that spirit analyses itself, distinguishes its moments, and halts at each individual mode in turn. The isolating of such moments presupposes

spirit itself and requires spirit for its subsistence, in other words, this isolation of modes only exists within spirit, which is existence.[18]

The "previous mode" called self-consciousness (which explores desire, struggle, lordship and bondage, stoicism, skepticism, and the unhappy consciousness) does not treat complete historical phenomena. Rather, it isolates the self-conscious efforts of individuals to understand themselves.[19] As such it abstracts from the total context of relations, which define and determine individuals in their real existence.

It is in the search for unquestionable and assured knowledge that the *Phenomenology of Spirit* analyzes its sequence of stages. Each claim to certainty is tested against its implicit truth. When they do not correspond, that claim collapses and becomes transformed into a subsequent, more inclusive one.[20] At the level of spirit, certainty claims that the social context must be understood before knowledge is possible. In contrast, at the level of self-consciousness, the individual claims that truth will be attained if one focuses simply on oneself. The truth claim of the natural order is ignored, as well as the truth claim of any other person.[21] From the broader perspective of spirit we can recognize this as but an isolated and abstract moment within the total picture. The individual's eyes, however, are closed to that broader perspective.

Thus the discussion of stoicism examines that type of consciousness which seeks truth about itself in pure, simple thought, isolated from its relations to the legal and political world. But stoicism as an historical movement covered more than this individualistic concern. It made political claims which set the individual in a larger context. This broader setting is considered in the section on legal status.[22]

We turn back to unhappy consciousness with a clearer picture of its role in the *Phenomenology*. Baillie's suggestion that its background is the "mental attitude assumed under the dominion of the Roman Catholic Church and the Feudal Hierarchy" suggests too much. The ecclesiastical and social structures of the Middle Ages make up the total cultural setting of an historical period. They cover far more than the individual, abstracted from his social context, who seeks truth simply about himself. The section on self-consciousness is concerned only with the latter, more limited, phenomenon.[23]

II

A question still remains. We noted earlier that the life-and-death struggle for recognition cannot recur in developed societies. There is a sense in which it is unrepeatable, even though it is abstract. Is this also true for unhappy consciousness? Does it specifically refer to the psychology of medieval Catholicism? Or is it a phenomenon which is found at different times, and is in principle repeatable, like that of slave-consciousness? For we have suggested that both abstractness *and* repeatability are conditions for a universal characteristic of human experience. To answer the question of repeatability specifically we need to know the basic structure of unhappy consciousness's experience.

In Hegel's analysis,[24] this stage arises out of skepticism. The skeptical distrust of any truth claim acknowledges universal denial to be its implicit truth. The universality of that claim comes to consciousness, however, only when skepticism is left behind. Even then it is present, not as fully achieved, but as yet to be attained. On the one hand, unhappy consciousness retains the experience of skepticism, aware of itself as changing and inconstant, fluctuating with every new thought or event. But on the other hand, unlike skepticism, it is certain that thereby it has missed the essential moment of truth. The unchanging and secure essence lies beyond—present in consciousness only as a yearning for that which it lacks.

Hegel explores the experience of individuals who seek to appropriate unchanging truth by transcending their own changing inconstancy. Since they are aware of themselves simply as changing, the reconciliation only becomes possible if the initiative comes from beyond—from the unchanging. For the unhappy consciousness, the unchanging essence takes on distinct forms—forms which provide a bridge over the ugly broad ditch between time and eternity. Not only does the unchanging stand absolutely opposed to the individual's fluctuating consciousness; it also assumes on its own the particular structure of individuality—a structure which it shares with the yearning seeker. This specific union of individual particularity with the unchanging only *represents* the desired integration. In its third form the unchanging allows the changing consciousness itself to be taken into a reconciled life. As external beyond, as changing individual, and as achieved reconciliation the unchanging appears to the unhappy consciousness. But the appearance as a form of the unchanging is not yet its fully realized experience within the alienated consciousness. To appropriate that promise the individual selves, on their part, have to overcome the changeable and insecure character of their own lives. Since the experienced reconciliation is yet to be achieved, it is the second, individual, form of the unchanging which becomes the focus of their attention. For it is the agent by means of which the culminating experience is to become manifest.

Hegel outlines three progressive stages of consciousness' quest to overcome its changeable nature. The first incorporates the response of devotion. Self-consciousness turns directly towards the individual form of the unchanging and absorbs that awareness into its own intellect. Disdaining any effort to comprehend by reflective thought, it surrenders itself to the immediacy of intellectual feeling or intuition.

The attitude of devotion, however, does not overcome the alienation. On the one hand, the unchanging as individual still lies beyond and outside of the devotee. The only concrete evidence available is a grave, empty of the living essence of eternal truth. On the other hand, the changing self has achieved only its own immediate feeling of devotion which, it discovers, is condemned to fluctuate and vanish. It has not transcended change.

The second stage of unhappy consciousness, then, turns not outward towards an objective embodiment of the unchanging, but inward into its own awareness of itself. Its own desire and labor are to be the means of reconciliation. Earlier in the *Phenomenology*, primitive self-consciousness through desire and the servant through labor, achieved positive certainty about themselves. At this stage, however, those who desire and labor are alienated from themselves. As a result these two ways of functioning share in their alienation and reflect their fundamental lack of self-certainty. They do not desire that which will immediately satisfy the senses, but consume the natural world to appropriate thereby the unchanging. Labor does not reproduce an objective expression of the self's activity, but rather seeks to reproduce that which will escape decay.

Desire and labor can achieve the desired reconciliation only if the unchanging allows itself to be appropriated and embodied through them. For the alienated individuals, then, the reality which is desired and the actions to be performed already participate in the unchanging essence of all things. Indeed their own instincts and capacities are effective only because they too have been made powerful through the initiative of the unchanging. When this comes fully to consciousness, the individuals can only give thanks. For both the material, desired and worked upon, and the ability, to appropriate and embody, have been received from beyond.

The culminating act of thanksgiving, however, has been undertaken as their own personal response. They are thrown back once again into their remaining independence, still condemned to be alienated from the truth. In the third stage of unhappy consciousness they seek to divest themselves completely of any remaining self-conscious initiative.

At this point everything the changing selves do consciously is valueless. Instead of rejoicing in their own activity—even in their animal functions—they mourn, for such actions condemn them to their separate, changing existence. All initiative must come from else-where. The individualized form of the unchanging essence, which started as the object of devotion and became the sacramental world of desire and labor, is now the mediator who alone can act with positive effect and accomplish the reconciliation. The changing individuals self-consciously transfer the guilt of their own acts, as changing, to the mediator. And in return they receive from the mediator direction concerning what they are to do. In total obedience the individuals surrender the positive value of self-determination. Even their own satisfaction in achievement must be sacrificed. They are told to use meaningless formulae, to confiscate the products of their own labor, to abstain from eating, and to mutilate their bodies. The determinate content of their action, together with the satisfaction of achievement belong not to the changing self-consciousness, but to the unchanging.

In this third stage of self-mortification, the unhappy conscious-ness finally transcends its changing, isolated individuality. Its deeds are but an instance of the universal activity of the unchanging media-tor. As far as it is aware, this universal act is still that of a beyond, not of itself. If it were to become fully conscious of the unchanging uni-versal as the truth of its own activity, it would have transcended the isolation of its self-concerned individuality and recognized that rea-son is common to both self and world. Reason, then, is the stage which Hegel will examine next in the *Phenomenology*.

III

Unhappy consciousness has as its object the three forms of the unchanging: external beyond, changing individual, and achieved rec-onciliation. Its subjective life is characterized by the three attitudes of devotion, sacramental desire and labor, and self-mortification. This double triad provides the schema for this stage of human development.

As Baillie suggests, individual Catholics in the Middle Ages may have embodied this pattern in their personal faith—the devotion directed toward the saints, the Virgin, or Jesus himself; the sacramen-tal sacrifice and communion of the Eucharist;[25] and the self-mortifica-tion of the ascetic hermits. Is this, however, the full range of applica-tion for Hegel's analysis? Are the three experiential stages repeated elsewhere, or are they retained only as part of our cultural memory?

Hegel himself provides a reminiscence of this structure within the section "Belief and Pure Insight" later in the *Phenomenology*—a discus-sion that recalls both the medieval period and the Age of Enlighten-ment.[26] And he makes explicit reference to unhappy consciousness as a necessary condition for the appearance of revealed religion.[27] However, both passages consider the Christian tradition: one, within a social context that includes its cultural counterpart; the other, as it provides the locus for the revelation of absolute truth.

If the absolute, when revealed, can be known by individuals, they must have within their own consciousness and life a capacity to comprehend which corresponds to that which is to be comprehended.[28] This capacity, Hegel suggests, is centered in "the yearning agony of the unhappy despairing self-consciousness."[29] If the truth to be known is absolute and complete, the capacity to know must also be universal—implicit in all conscious individuals. We might, then, expect to find manifestations of unhappy consciousness in historical contexts other than those which are specifically Christian.

We have already noticed that Jewish religion, the economic structure of the ancient world, and the political pattern of oriental despotism provided concrete historical settings for the type of consciousness analyzed in lordship and bondage. By analogy we may infer that unhappy consciousness will be found in contexts which, though roughly contemporary with the appearance of Christianity, are yet distinct from it. The influx of oriental religions into Rome during the second and third centuries in fact does provide such an alternative setting.

While there is little literary documentation for the religious psychology underlying that movement,[30] there is evidence to suggest that the devotee of these religions, yearning for immortality, is an instance of changing consciousness seeking reconciliation with the unchangeable. In Attis or Osiris, the unchangeable takes on the form of a man or god, who in dying manifests its identity with the changeable.[31] The cult of the dying and rising god becomes the context for the joy of experienced reconciliation. There are, then, clear parallels to the three forms of the unchanging essence.

From Cumont's description we can reconstruct some elements of a second-century Roman's personal experience. In the first place, the initiates may devote their individual attention to the divinity in pure adoration: "During the entire forenoon, from the moment that a noisy acclamation had greeted the rising of the sun, the images of the gods [Isis and Osiris/Serapis] were exposed to the silent adoration of the initiates."[32]

Secondly, they may eat a cultic meal, or purify themselves by means of ritual baths. "Frequent sacred repasts maintained a spirit of fellowship among the mystics of Cybele, Mithra or the Baals." And "a series of ablutions and lustrations [were] supposed to restore original innocence to the mystic."[33]

In the third place,

> purgation of the soul was not effected solely by liturgic acts
> but also by self-denial and suffering.... Macerations, laborious
> pilgrimages, public confessions, sometimes flagellations and
> mutilations, in fact all forms of penance and mortifications
> uplifted the fallen man and brought him nearer to the gods.[34]

In addition,

> it was the priest's prerogative to judge the misdeeds and to
> impose the penalties.... The priest was no longer simply the
> guardian of sacred traditions, the intermediary between man
> or the state and the gods, but also a spiritual guide. He taught
> his flock the long series of obligations and restrictions for
> shielding their weakness from the attacks of evil spirits. He
> knew how to quiet remorse and scruples, and to restore the
> sinner to spiritual calm. Being versed in sacred knowledge, he
> had the power of reconciling the gods.[35]

Initiates into Syrian cults learned the magic incantations by which
they might satisfy the divinity. And in the more enthusiastic religions
of Asia Minor devotees would mouth ecstatic utterances, unintelligi-
ble even to themselves.

When one places Hegel's analysis of religious psychology beside
the detailed account of oriental religions in second century Rome provided by Cumont, one suspects that historians might well consider
the dynamics of unhappy consciousness in their efforts to explain
those developments. Indeed, one may infer that Hegel is directly concerned with this period of Roman history, disenchanted with stoicism, threatened by skepticism, entranced by oriental religions and
infiltrated by Christianity; not with that later, medieval church, which
shared in the stability of the feudal order.

In the doctrine and practice of Buddhism we find a second historical instance of unhappy consciousness. Nirvana, not immortality, is
the unchanging for the Buddhist:

> We may have, O priests, the case of one who, himself subject
> to birth, perceives the wretchedness of what is subject to
> birth, and craves the incomparable security of a Nirvana free
> from birth; himself subject to old age..., disease..., death...,
> sorrow..., corruption, perceives the wretchedness of what is
> subject to corruption, and craves the incomparable security of
> a Nirvana free from corruption.[36]

In Mahayana thought, this unchangeable essence takes on concrete forms: "The Body of Essence, the Body of Bliss, the Transformation Body—these are the bodies of the Buddhas." The Body of Essence, "uniform and subtle," corresponds to the pure unchanging, the Transformation Body, which "displays with skill birth, enlightenment, and Nirvana, for it possesses much magic power to lead men to enlightenment," is the individual form of the unchanging as agent of reconciliation. The Body of Bliss which "varies in all the planes of the Universe according to region, in name, in form, and in experience of phenomena" represents the ecstatic union of the individual consciousness with eternal truth.[37]

Hegel's three levels of religious experience fit, although awkwardly, with the eightfold path. The first two steps, right belief and right resolve, introduce a preliminary focusing of the mind and will on the eternal truth.[38] Often this is nurtured through silent meditation in a temple, responding to the pervasive influence of a statue of Buddha immersed in inner contemplation. Right speech, right behavior, and right occupation take up the pattern of the sacramental life in which desire and labor are given transcendental significance. The middle way of moderation, and the discipline of the Sangha (or order of monks) are concrete embodiments of this stage.[39] Finally, the culminating stages of right effort, right contemplation, and right concentration direct the initiates to divest their minds of all concrete desires, and all concrete thoughts:

Whenever, O priests, a priest, having isolated himself from sensual pleasures, having isolated himself from demeritorious traits, and still exercising reasoning, still exercises reflection, enters upon the first trance which is produced by isolation and characterized by joy and happiness; when, through the subsidence of reasoning and reflection, and still retaining joy and happiness, he enters upon the second trance, which is an interior tranquilization and intentness of the thoughts and is produced by concentration; when, through the paling of joy, indifferent, contemplative, conscious, and in the experience of bodily happiness—that state which eminent men describe when they say, "Indifferent, contemplative, and living happily"—he enters upon the third trance; when through the abandonment of misery, through the disappearance of all antecedent gladness and grief, he enters upon the fourth trance, which has neither misery nor happiness, but is contemplation as refined by indifference, this, O priests, is called 'right concentration'.[40]

These words of direction and advice come from the Lord, Gautama Buddha himself, who thus takes the initiative for the content of the believer's individual actions.[41]

The abstract terms used in the chapter on unhappy consciousness seem to apply not only to the quest for immortality in second century Rome, but also to the yearning for Nirvana in traditional Buddhism.[42] Hegel has avoided specific historical reference lest he direct the reader's attention away from the more universal relevance of his analysis. In our third example, we suggest that the individual psychology of unhappy consciousness is not simply a cultural memory from the past, but is a recent phenomenon.[43]

The skepticism of the 1970s stemmed from our knowledge of historical change and diversity. Claims to certainty were taken to be but the expression of a psychological need or the result of sociological conditioning, lacking truth. In this context young people turned to religious perspectives that promised personal security and a way of transcending the world of change, doubt, and cosmic despair. Hindu cults and Buddhist literature vied with Christian pre-millennial sects for the individual's attention and commitment. The alienation of the unhappy consciousness, however, also pervaded the realm of political concern and action,[44] and some took up Marxism, not as a scientific theory of explanation, but as a way of transcending the agony of contemporary insecurity and despair.

We can only sketch the parallels. The necessity of the historical dialectic was the eternal unchanging which stood over against the fluctuating dynamic of rapid social change. The necessity was present concretely in the theoretical analyses of Karl Marx, in the achievements of Communist China, or in the potential of the exploited proletariat. The individual aspired to be reconciled with dialectical necessity in the classless society.

Devotion appeared when individuals contemplated the various embodiments of the unchanging truth with an intellectual attitude that accepted without critical reflection. It came to grief in the realization that there were significant events in the world which could not be explained directly from the texts, that China was not a paradise on earth, and that the proletariat manifested characteristics far more complex and ambiguous than pure theory suggested.

Consciousness could then claim that the universality of the historical dialectic was immanent within the total dynamic of social and political life, and could be appropriated only through specific desires and actions. Life in a commune anticipated the classless society. Political action in one's place of work sought to reproduce dialectical necessity. These acts, however, could reconcile individuals with what is ultimately significant in history only if the implacable dialectic so determined it. They had thought to be participants in the classless society through their own initiatives. Experience taught them that they were totally insignificant, and their initiatives had no determining effect on the course of events.

So, finally, individuals were prepared to sacrifice themselves to this ultimate goal, even if that sacrifice was completely useless. They sought to initiate violent revolution, though they were aware that the result might well be their own deaths, and a despotic regime of reactionary repression. They followed blindly the one who, professing to know Marxist theory, directed the action of the revolutionary cell. And they mouthed the cant phrases of propaganda which had lost any value as informative speech.[45]

Marxism, like Christianity and Buddhism, included much more than this one dimension of individual psychology. It may be, as Hegel suggests, that this quest for reconciliation with ultimate security anticipates within the individual psyche the structure of universal truth. Despite Hegel, however, we are not certain that absolute knowledge is attainable. Therefore such a possibility can only be proposed, not established as the truth.

Our more limited goal, however, has been attained. The parallels suggested between unhappy consciousness and the phenomena of oriental religions in the Roman empire, of Buddhism, and of contemporary Marxism provide some support for the conclusion that Hegel, in this section of the *Phenomenology*, is not simply concentrating on medieval Catholicism. He uses an abstract vocabulary and analyzes the individual self-consciousness, isolated from its historical context, because the experience of the unhappy consciousness is universal. It is a perennial possibility in human nature, reappearing in the lives of individuals even in our day.

We can conclude, then, that Baillie's suggestions and footnotes are misleading. Hegel does not have in mind "the forms assumed in European history." He is consciously analyzing "an experience that is strictly found in all mankind."[46] Indeed, from this limited study we are encouraged to make a stronger claim. The *Phenomenology* is not primarily a philosophy of history. Despite its analysis of developmental stages, it more closely approximates traditional epistemology. For it seeks to outline the universal conditions necessary for any knowledge whatsoever. Despite the confident assumptions of the Enlightenment and its heirs, the alienation of unhappy consciousness is, for Hegel, one of those conditions.

XI

God, Man, and Death
in Hegel's Phenomenology

In an appendix to his *Introduction à la lecture de Hegel* Kojève contrasts the Christian religion to Hegel's historical humanism as positive to negative:

> In the final analysis, the God of Christian theology (of ancient and pagan inspiration) is given-Being [*Sein*], eternally identical to itself and revealing itself in and through a natural world, which only manifests the essence and the power of existing of a Being that *is*. The Man of Hegel, on the contrary, is the *Nothingness* [*Nichts*] that annihilates given-Being existing as World, and that annihilates itself (as real historical time or History) in and through that annihilation of the given.[1]

As Kojève realized, man's negativity is most critically present in death. For death is not only the ultimate limit of natural life; man can consciously anticipate, and indeed may freely choose, death. But Kojève's wide-ranging exposition of this thesis is limited in its reference to some passages in the preface to the *Phenomenology*. Only in conclusion does he illustrate his point with earlier writings from the Jena period, and from the life-and-death struggle.

For Hegel, however, the substance of his philosophical position is not to be found in the more relaxed discussion of the preface. It is the text itself of the *Phenomenology* that carries the weight of his argument. There one indeed finds death playing a crucial role in the development towards absolute knowing. Not only the life-and-death struggle and the slave are marked by the stark evidence of mortality, but also unhappy consciousness, the ethical order, absolute freedom and terror, and revealed religion.

By looking at each of these sections in turn, we can begin to articulate the ways in which death and negativity serve as necessary conditions for knowledge. Such a discussion will not only add substantial support for Kojève's thesis regarding the essential negativity of man's historical existence, but will invert his conclusion by showing that, far from alienating man from God, the centrality of death is the necessary condition for a complete reconciliation.

I

In the most primitive form of self-consciousness that Hegel isolates, the self is not yet aware of its own mortality.[2] Its environment presents no unsurpassable limit to its dynamic activity, but is rather the object of desire—raw material to be appropriated into its indeterminate and all-inclusive living reality.

This expansive totality meets its limit in another self who has the same view of the world.[3] Since neither self will allow the other to appropriate it, a struggle results—a struggle whose inherent motivation will be satisfied only where one or both of the combatants dies.

In Hegel's analytical reconstruction of experience, this moment of death marks the first point at which an individual consciousness becomes aware of its finitude and of its limitations. What was taken to be limitless is discovered to have inescapable boundaries. For it matters not what one intends to achieve if one dies. Therefore death can here be called the first negation that becomes present in the experience of self-consciousness.

Self-consciousness, however, does not simply come to an end. Because its basic desire extends beyond what it is already, it can anticipate what is to come. When it knows that death is possible—that a radical limitation can in fact be imposed—it can seek to cancel that inevitability. Since such a move endeavours to negate finitude, it can be called the second negation—or the negation of negation. In its most primitive form this transition takes place when one combatant realizes his vulnerability, and instead of continuing to the bitter end, surrenders and becomes a slave of the other.[4]

This is not the last word, however, for the consciousness of death on the part of the slave transforms the second negation into something positive. For in having his self-certainty shaken to the core, he becomes aware of himself as living process, not as enduring essence, and discovers that the products of his labor embody the dynamic activity that constitutes his life.[5] The finitude that was first acknowledged only through the threat of death is no longer known as a bare limitation, but rather as a positive and determinate character. The third negation cancels the negativity of the previous two moments and allows their positive import to become evident. The fear of death, the sovereign master, is the beginning of wisdom.

Throughout this development, death is present as something that happens to the self—a threat produced by another self-consciousness. It is, to that extent, conditioned and cannot generate pure self-knowledge. On the other hand, as the slave realized, to die, even at one's own hand, is to cancel all possibilities. This results in a double tension in self-consciousness. To achieve pure knowledge one must pass beyond one's limitations, but one cannot end one's life. Therefore one has to overcome those elements of life that manifest finitude.

This happens in the stage of unhappy consciousness, where the self knows itself as changing, and attempts to cancel this changing character so that it can be reconciled with the unchanging.[6] This involves self-mortification. While there is here no physical death, the self consciously attempts to exterminate its individuality. In this process the first negation is the finitude of change and decay which is not consciously produced but consciously acknowledged. The second negation is the process of self-mortification, but the third negation is the awareness that the mediated process of self-mortification is the concrete dynamic of unchanging reality itself. This opens up the perspective of reason.[7]

II

The section of the *Phenomenology* that discusses the master-slave relationship and the unhappy consciousness focuses on the individual self, abstracted from its social context. But humans are social beings, and they come of age, not as individuals in an indifferent world, but as integrated members of a mature society. The social and historical dimension of our maturity is explored by Hegel in his discussion of spirit, where he talks not about individuals conscious of themselves, but about the characteristic ethos of a people.[8] At this stage death reappears as a significant theme.

In the immediacy of its primitive cultural ethos, a people finds that there is a tension between the divine law inherent in the family or clan, and the human law of social organization.[9] On both sides of the tension, death has a role to play. On the one hand, the divinity inherent in the family bonds achieves universality only when, through death, the finitude of relatives and ancestors has been dissolved. Here death is not the first negation. That is rather the particularity of diverse, living individuals. By cancelling individuality, death negates that negation, allowing the inherent divine law to become self-contained as a universally significant (but dark and shadowy) force in human society.[10]

On the other hand, the contrary human law maintains its authority by threatening death and by reminding citizens of their inherent limitations. "In order not to let them get rooted and settled in their isolation and thus break up the whole into fragments and let the common spirit evaporate, government has from time to time to shake them to the very centre in war."[11] By forcing individuals to feel the power of their lord and master, the government uses death as a first negation, reminding them of their finitude so that they will transcend its limitations by participating in the public life of the community.

In Hegel's discussion, the archetype of this conflict between the two laws is found in Sophocles' *Antigone*.[12] When Oedipus, the king of Thebes, dies, he leaves behind two sons who, as brothers, are bound by the divine law of the family. Since they cannot both share in the royal power they agree to take turns. When, at the end of his term, the elder refuses to transfer authority because of his seniority, the other, grounding his claim on the original agreement, initiates a struggle. No longer a personal dispute, it becomes a war, for the rebel enlists the support of neighbouring states. After both brothers die in personal combat, the new monarch, as punishment, refuses to grant the rebel the proper rite of burial. In the person of Antigone, the divine law of the family challenges this decree of human law. In response the human law condemns her to death. But her protest awakens the consciousness that it is the divine law that sanctions oaths and establishes the positive unity of the community. At first bloodless and ineffectual, it opens up the possibility of the civil order dissolving and of justified retribution by other communities, so the government has to surrender. In this denouement, human law is weakened by its lack of independent authority, while divine law is shown to be impotent, unable to translate its universal bond adequately into the discrete decisions of civil society.

The two roles that death plays here intersect and interact. The punishment of the criminal's corpse both defines his finitude and translates his cause into a bloodless universality. The resulting struggle that threatens to become a war both redefines the authority of the civil government and marks its demise. The conflict, thus archetypically represented, results in the inexorable dissolution of the power of both divine and human law, replacing them with the abstract individualism of legal personality. The fateful movement of destiny through the medium of death dissolves the contradiction between the two laws into an abstract unity—a result that only formally embodies the third logical moment in which a second negation is cancelled so that a positive may emerge.

Hegel's subsequent discussion of spirit estranged from itself takes place in the abstracted realm of culture. As such it is not concerned with the immediate reality of death. Hegel signals this loss by noting that the counsellor, who serves culture's "realm of actuality," would give sound—universally valid—advice were he prepared to surrender his particular interests to the point of death.[13] When he pulls back, however, he falls into the attitude of flattery in which he only reaffirms his changing, contingent, and finite individuality.

In the unreal world of pure speech that results, the debate between pure insight and faith, between enlightenment and superstition, takes place.[14] Faith represents in its objective doctrine the death of a finite individual who also is God. But its subjective response is a positive trust or acceptance of that dogma. In contrast, the enlightenment subjectively actualizes the negative dynamic through constant criticism; it destroys all reference to a beyond by showing the inherent finitude and limitation of the faith that is supposed to be universal. Yet death itself is not objectively affirmed, only the positive reality of the present. Ironically each embodies subjectively what the other affirms objectively.

The negative practice of the enlightenment, however, is not limited to the cut and thrust of debate. It challenges individual finitude in order to show that what is important is the universal. When it turns to nature and the social order, anything that is determinate and particular is shown to be simply useful. Its value is derived not from its positive reality, but from its negative role as passing over to something more comprehensive. In the last analysis only negatively active subjects who are "enlightened" agents are inherently valuable in their own right.

This is the structure of absolute freedom. When all independent ideas have been demolished, the enlightenment continues to actualise itself only by venturing into overt action. Nothing is conceded that would limit the negative capacity to use. Everything is simply grist for its mill, lacking independent reality.

Absolute freedom only knows how to say: No! But now the only thing that continues to resist its universal ability to use things for its own purpose is the negative activity of other individuals. To say No! to such action is to send the agent to his or her death.[15]

Once again, then, death becomes an important condition for the advance to absolute knowing—death that is chosen in absolute freedom. And once again it performs three different functions, all negative, but ordered in sequence.

The first negation is the single willed decision to condemn to death. For the exercise of freedom, as a specific act, is finite and particular.

The purpose of absolute freedom, however, is to dissolve just such resistant finitude. For it is the positive determination of individual activity that is to be destroyed. Therefore the reign of terror develops as one after another, ignoring the finitude of his or her own decisions, condemns it in others.

If the *decision* to condemn to death is the first negation, its execution is the second, for finitude and particularity are thereby cancelled. However, the third negation follows from the absolute character of the free act. Since freedom's purpose is to exterminate all recalcitrant individuality, it is its own free act that it wills to destroy. The self-confidence of pure freedom dissipates into absolute fear. No longer is this the slave's fear of that which is alien, unknown, or independent; it is terror before the fact that, in absolute freedom, one is choosing one's own death. And in contrast to the universality of the divine law, there is here no beyond into which one's individuality can disappear. For it was destroyed by enlightenment's victory over faith.

This moment of pure self-knowledge generates the third negation. Not only is human finitude actualized, not only is that finitude cancelled; but by bringing the two together so that pure self-knowledge knows that it wills its own death through its own inherent activity, the terror of absolute annihilation opens up. Shaken to its roots, the bacchanalian revel of purely negative activity collapses into a transparent and simple calm.[16] For at this point man becomes aware of the positive fact he is free to create *ex nihilo*, and the prospect of genuinely moral action opens up.

By consciously dwelling with the negativity of the terror, spirit knows itself as it is, not only as able to use everything in self-contained freedom, but also as the inherently negative power of destruction, and therefore of genuine creativity. Implicit in the divine law of the family and in the willed decision of human government, present in the irony of enlightenment's struggle against superstition, this its own inherent reality now becomes explicitly acknowledged and comprehended. Apart from this self-knowledge, the political animal appeals either to the irony of history or to the inexorable laws of the social order to explain what happens, and in either case denies its responsibility. With it, a political organization of rationally free people becomes possible.

Through the demise of the city-state in which the contradictory roles of death dissolve the social order, through the superficiality of a culture that endeavours to ignore death, and through the trauma of the reign of terror, men and women come to the level of self-awareness that recognizes how they, as individuals come of age, are integrated with a society that has come of age.

III

As Kojève suggests, death is a necessary condition for reaching human maturity. The contradictory trauma of the reign of terror turns upside down to ground the coming of age of modern man and woman. But does this mean that they thereby become alienated from God—that the simple positivity of religious belief is simply left behind? For when the products of Enlightenment have become fully confident in their own powers and have accepted the radical creativity that lies within their own freedom, they would seem to have no further need of transcendent and supernatural powers.

Even were we simply to reflect on the passages already discussed, we would soon realize that, for Hegel, religion is not a matter of simple positive dogma and faith. For in the discussion of master and slave, where Hegel talks of death as the sovereign master, he evokes themes from the Old Testament with its assertion that the fear of the Lord is the beginning of wisdom. Indeed in his lectures on history and religion Hegel refers to this relationship when talking of Judaism or of the claim to divinity in oriental and Roman despotism.[17] Similarly, in a primitive cultural ethos, the law of the family immortalized in the dead is called the divine law and indeed contrasted with the positivity of the human law. Finally, the dogmatic content of faith pictures the death of God even though it asserts it positively.

Even so it is possible that those more primitive levels of superstition could be dissolved with the arrival of the modern world, were it not for the fundamental tension inherent in the latter achievement. For the moral autonomy of radical creativity, which generates its own laws, is bivalent. On the one hand it asserts our self-sufficient independence as being solely responsible for what we have become. On the other it discovers that we are still conditioned products of our environment—of the location in time and space where we are thrown into existence. The universe itself is seen as indifferent to our moral courage, such that our efforts to do good turn out to generate evil—so much so that we cannot forgive ourselves. Therefore we have attained neither absolute freedom nor comprehensive knowledge. Instead we are either presumptuous in asserting our ultimate dignity even as our insignificant existence is being bypassed by an indifferent and impersonal world, or deluded into taking our partial perspective as the key to all truth.

It is this experience of the very ones who have achieved historical maturity that requires Hegel's transition from the heights of moral responsibility to the perspective of religion. For religion is that sphere of human life in which we acknowledge the essential limitations of human nature, and open ourselves to the beyond that transcends such limitations. The self-surrender of devotion, however, would leave our finitude unresolved were the divine simply to introduce a positive counterpoint to our negativity. Our ultimate reconciliation with our cosmic limitations will be achieved only if both sides—divine and human—embody the same dynamic structure. The central significance of Christianity for Hegel lies in the fact that, long before the traumatic achievements of modern autonomy, its dogma reported that God himself had in fact become a finite man and had died. In other words, the radical negativity of self-chosen death is also affirmed to be a central constituent of the divine life.[18]

The central Christian doctrine of the Incarnation presents the divine initiative as passing through three stages that reproduce the first, the second, and the third negation. In the first, God limits himself and becomes finite—an individual man specifically located in space and time. In the second, this individual dies; his finitude is cancelled. In the third, the negative force of his death is dissolved, and he becomes universally present as the resurrected Christ.

In this deposit of faith, the Christian is told that the negativity of death is an integral part of divinity—that the universe itself embodies the structure of triple negation. But the information thus communicated is not appropriated in a way that comprehends the significance of what is involved. At one time, the response is that of unhappy consciousness, which believes that the history of salvation introduces no change or process in God himself and which tries only to overcome its own changing impermanence through self-mortification. There is here no recognition of how essential the negativity of change and transformation is to a complete reconciliation. At another time the Christian response is faith, the object of enlightenment's derision. It accepts the doctrine as given, simply asserting it to be true on the basis of positive authority, whether scripture, miracles, or church. In both unhappy consciousness and faith there is no ultimate reconciliation between the human and the divine, because our subjective response embodies characteristics contrary to those presented in the divine history.

Following Luther, and in German pietism, however, a third response develops, which recognizes that the appropriation of divine reality comes by way of an existential dynamic involving the Christian community. This dynamic does not happen simply in the self-consciousness of the Christian believer. It requires as its necessary condition the dogmatic representation of the history of salvation. This happens in three stages.[19]

First, Christian theology says that God created the world out of nothing and in this world created humans in his own image. Since God was not limited by an alien matter, there is nothing inherent that would absolutely frustrate a reconciliation. The human and the divine, however, are not identical; for men and women are finite, whereas God is thought to be infinite and complete. When finite men and women seek to become self-contained and independent as he is thought to be, they break apart the homogeneous fabric of the universe and introduce the difference between good and evil. For evil is the self-contained refusal to allow oneself to be incorporated into the larger totality.

Human nature, as self-contained finitude, is inherently evil. But when this story is appropriated in the Christian community, self-conscious believers become aware of themselves as evil, and their agony and despair increase.[20] For they know themselves to be absolutely other than divine reality.

In this first stage, death is simply the evidence of our finitude, the "wages of sin." When, in the doctrinal story of the Fall, self-centered and independent humans isolate themselves and thus transform their limits into an absolute limitation or barrier, they render themselves radically finite; death, as the first negation, actualizes that finitude. However, the Christian community's self-conscious awareness of its own inherent sin focuses on this first negation as its object, and in so doing takes its distance, implicitly introducing the second negation. As yet, however, this is only inherent, not fully developed in consciousness.

In the second stage, Christian doctrine represents the self-emptying initiative of divine reality in becoming a man and in dying so that human nature and its evil might be reconciled with God.[21] His death is, as we have seen, confirmation of the radical finitude of the incarnate one. But in the context of the Christian community it is given a contrary sense. Rather than being the first negation of limitation, it is the second; it cancels particularity and finitude so that the incarnate one continues to live universally. Not limited by space and time, he dies and is raised again daily in the worship and devotion of the Christian community.

The Christian believers thus become conscious of the fact that the reconciliation is already achieved. The second negation that was only implicit in the consciousness of evil here becomes explicitly acknowledged and affirmed. For this story of salvation lets them know that, through the divine initiative, the confession of sin has become a necessary condition for atonement, making it possible. However, complete reconciliation, which would transform the cancelling of sin's limitation into a dynamic positive community of spiritual life, is only present in principle. It has not yet become explicit in believing consciousness. That is achieved only in the third stage of revealed religion.

The final integration of the human with the divine comes about because the religious consciousness acknowledges that the total dynamic of the reconciling events takes place in the living consciousness of the Christian community.[22] It is universally present only because it is thought and appropriated by the believing self. But as this becomes self-consciously articulated, new levels of awareness appear. In the first place, as we have seen, the self-contained independence of the mediator's objective life is dissolved into the universal dynamic of Christian self-consciousness. In the second place, it is through this self-consciousness that the promise of the spirit to the Christian community, contained in Christian doctrine, leaves the abstract world of thought and becomes actual. However, in the third place, the believer realizes that there no longer remains a transcendent divine reality that is independent and self-contained, above and beyond human existence. For that has been dissolved in the incarnation and death of the mediator. And when the believers open themselves totally in worship and devotion, they do not encounter a God out there, but only themselves. They are overwhelmed by the dark night of the soul, in which each as conscious ego encounters only his or her self. They realize that God himself has died. While radically conscious of their own evil, believers find no beyond to provide a remedy. This trauma marks their spiritual death, for their particularity expires into the abyss of meaninglessness, and no solid substantial foundation remains in which to trust.

At first this is the second negation, for it cancels the positive universality of the hoped-for reconciliation and transforms it into the negative subjectivity of an intensely personal dynamic. It runs through the moments from hope to despair as it appropriates existentially the content of what is presented dogmatically and transcends its positive form. But in fact it is the third negation. For this dynamic, which both reaches out to what is independent, incorporating it into one's life, and surrenders one's own independence, has become identical in finite humans and in God. The painful awareness of the death of God allows the spiritual integration of the human with the divine not only in dogmatic theory but in actual fact. In other words, in the revealed religion of Christianity God is negatively defined as dying, not only in the objective content of its positive doctrine, but in the subjective, existential consciousness of the believer. And when this takes place death does not just define the limits of our finitude, nor cancel the mediator's particularity, but it reveals the fundamental identity of the human and the divine. Both become actual by negatively dissolving the negativity through which their negatively determined isolation (whether abstract beyond or self-contained evil) is cancelled.

When one lives in a reconciled relation with God, then, God ceases to be wholly other and is present in the spiritual community that incorporates both God and finite spirit. Since such a community requires the active participation of both the divine and the human partners, the negative death of God as abstract other has converted into the positive presence of God as spirit.

Until this final move is acknowledged and articulated through the self-conscious comprehension of thought, we have not achieved absolute knowledge.[23] Only when we recognize that the negative dynamic that has radically defined human nature come of age is identical with the negative dynamic of manifest religion are we able to know that our secular experience is not a misleading delusion, but the achievement of maturity.

But does this mean that once such knowledge is achieved, we moderns can dispense with religion? If this were the case, Kojève's thesis would have some plausibility: not that our negativity dissolves God's positivity, but that God's negativity dissolves itself. Thus, come of age, we embody in our own humanity the truth of religion. There are reasons, however, why such a conclusion is not convincing. After all, Hegel consistently states that the result, abstracted from the process that leads to it, is false and misleading. The integration of the divine and the human can only be maintained if it continually incorporates within itself the total dynamic through which God dies and is yet affirmed to be present in human life. Once Feuerbach and others divorce our maturity from that which constitutes it, their assertions become finite and positivistic claims, not negatively comprehensive self-knowledge. For indeed Hegel is recapitulating in philosophical terms what Christians of profound faith have articulated throughout the ages; that the experience of personal reconciliation with God is the inversion of the experience of the death of God.[24]

Because Kojève does not acknowledge this, he is left with an unresolved historicism. For the ultimate question that needs to be answered if one is to distinguish between truth and historically conditioned opinion concerns the criterion that establishes one method or one way of self-definition as being the essential characteristic of the world as such. This, suggests Hegel, is only achieved in religious consciousness where the assertions of doctrine are not only accepted as true, but are appropriated through the dark night of the soul into the subjectivity of pure self-consciousness.

The preceding discussion of death throws light on negation in the Hegelian method.[25] For death is the most radical phenomenological evidence of negativity. In the first place a simple positive is negatively defined as something finite and limited. In this way it is rendered clear, precise, and determinate. In the second place, that limitation marks its own demise. Dialectic shows that the result is contradictory and must disappear. Its finitude is dissolved. In the third place, this negative conclusion is pushed to its most radical limits; its mediating ground is made evident, not as something static and independently determinate, but as dynamic and self-defining. No longer isolated from others, it is constantly interacting with them. This movement of three negations transforms the simple and immediate into a self-mediating process. Barely has the result appeared, however, than the negative process continues, defining, isolating, and rendering precise the result that has been achieved, taking it as an immediate to be rendered determinate. Thus no conclusion is final. It only opens up a new set of transitions.

Showing how this methodological principle is but the distilled essence of the total dynamic of human experience is the task of Hegel's *Phenomenology*. This is why death plays such an important role in its development.

XII

The Syllogisms of Revealed Religion

I

For the Enlightenment, a continuing question was the reasonableness of Christianity. John Locke devoted a treatise to the question; and it lies at the core of Hume's essay on miracles, of Lessing's ugly, broad ditch, and of Kant's religion within the limits of reason alone.

Therefore when Hegel uses the language of judgement and syllogism in characterizing the Christian doctrine of creation, fall, and redemption, it is not something to be passed over lightly. The logical terms suggest that Hegel has discovered an implicit rationality within the dogmas of Christian belief. When we compare the first edition of the *Encyclopedia* with the second and third, we find that this use of terms is deliberate.[1] For it was introduced into the later editions.

In the first edition revealed religion is characterized as the stage of reflection, between the immediate intuition of the religion of art and the self-conscious thinking of philosophy. And the three moments of God before creation, of creation and fall, and of redemption and reconciliation are distinguished as universality, particularity, and singularity. By the third edition a number of references to reflection have been removed, while others to the immediate unity of faith and devotion have been added. Judgement is much more directly identified with the moment of particularity. And the final paragraph (§571) begins with a new clause: "These three syllogisms, that constitute the *one* syllogism of the absolute mediation of spirit with itself are its revelation."

This reference to syllogism is new. Yet the two preceding paragraphs that are here summarized are not significantly altered. Apparently Hegel wanted to make explicit that his characterization of the

131

moment of redemption and reconciliation coincided with the logical patterns of syllogism and inference. He could thereby demonstrate the implicit rationality of revealed religion.

The cryptic text of the *Encyclopedia* leaves to the reader the task of comprehension. Hegel presumes familiarity with the logic of syllogism and expects that its application to revealed religion will be simply a question of instantiation. It might not be amiss, however, for an exegete to help the reader along by using the clues in §§569 and 570 to show what syllogisms they embody, and how they reflect rational operations. Such a task may throw light on the transition from revealed religion to philosophy—the culminating moment in the discussion of absolute spirit.

II

First, however, we need to review Hegel's discussion of the syllogisms.[2] Hegel's syllogistic structure is the form to which corresponds the content of an act of inference. It pictures the way two concepts or terms are brought together into a single perspective or judgement by means of a third term. And its focus hinges on the nature of this mediation.

The terms of a syllogism are conditioned by their conceptual status, which can be of three sorts. In the first place, there is an individual object of reference—a singular something that cannot be comprehended, but only indicated. In the second place there is a comprehensive generality or universality, an all-encompassing concept. In the third place there is the act of differentiating within this generality, of limiting it in terms of particular determination. The three terms in any syllogism must be distinguished from each other, then, by the way in which they embody these three characteristics: singular, universal, and particular. The mathematical syllogism, in which all three terms are universals, collapses into a bare, abstract tautology.

There are three basic syllogistic patterns. First, particularity mediates, connecting a singular and a universal [S-P-U]. Second, a singular mediates by synthesizing a particular and a universal [P-S-U]. Third, a universal mediates by distinguishing a singular and a particular [S-U-P].

This threefold pattern, expressed in terms of syllogism, is reproduced at another level in the nature of the inferential process involved. The first kind of process is simply a transition, passing over from one concept or term to a different one by way of a third. This transition to something other embodies the differentiating feature of particularity. Its most characteristic form is the Aristotelian Barbara syllogism: "Socrates is a man; men are mortal; so Socrates is mortal." The two transitions, from "Socrates" to "man" and from "men" to "mortal," from singular to particular and from particular to universal, are collapsed into a single, "differing" transition from a singular, "Socrates," to the universal "mortal."[3]

The second kind of inferential move is one in which a singular thought brings together a couple of concepts into a synthesis. This is the process of reflection—a process that tries to fit particular concepts into a more general context or theory. The paradigm case is induction, in which a particular set of cases is brought together to justify a general or universal claim. Since the set is not exhaustive, it represents particularity. And since the act of synthesis simply happens, it is a singular object of reference. Induction, however, presupposes another inferential move—the move of analogy, in which a singular reflection identifies a particular feature that it takes to be essential or universal as the justification for collecting just these singulars into its inductive set. While the inferential move in analogy is reflective and singular, the form of its operation is one in which the universal essence mediates between each singular and its particular set.

The third kind of inferential move is neither a simple transition nor a somewhat contingent synthesis, but a process of determining, of distinguishing within a universal its distinctive moments or features—its complementary yet differentiated functions. This finds its paradigm in a disjunctive syllogism in which a universal that includes a whole genus (in one premise) also excludes some particulars (in the other) to identify a singular (in the conclusion).

This sketch of Hegel's theoretical discussion of syllogism and inference provides background for Hegel's insertion of an explicit reference to three syllogisms into the paragraphs on religion. We now need to see how this formal structure is implicit in the characterization of revelation.

III

As already mentioned, Hegel develops the discussion of revealed religion through the three moments of universality, particularity, and singularity. God before creation is the self-determining universal that, like the self-contained process of conceiving, eternally differentiates (or particularizes) the Son from the Father while yet negating that negation to give God concrete individuality or singularity as spirit (§567). Creation and fall embody the particularizing act of judgement in which what is universal and what is determinate fall apart and are coupled only externally (§568). The third moment of redemption and reconciliation is to be singularity in contrast to universality and particularity—a complex network of relations that can only be indicated as a unit. Yet it is also to be the sphere of syllogism and inference, reintegrating the disruptive judgement into a single totality. To show how the complex of three syllogisms can yet be the moment of singularity we shall take each of the three in turn, analyze it in terms of the type of syllogism exemplified and the process of inference involved, and then consider how they may be seen as moments of a single syllogism that is "the absolute mediation of spirit with itself" (§571).

§569 c) In the moment of *singularity* as such, namely of subjectivity and of indeed the concept (as of the opposition of universality and particularity turned back into its *identical ground*) 1) the *universal* substance is displayed as *presupposition*, actualized out of its abstraction into *singular* self-consciousness, the latter as *immediately identical* with the essence—that son of the eternal sphere transplanted into temporality, evil as *inherently* sublated in him—yet further this immediate and hence sensuous existence of what is absolutely concrete [is displayed] placing itself into judgement and dying into the agony of negativity, through which as infinite subjectivity it has come to be identical with itself, out of subjectivity has come to be on its own account as *absolute return* and universal unity of the universal and singular essentiality—the Idea of spirit as eternal yet as *living* and present in the world.

In this first syllogism, the presupposition or starting point is an immediate, singular existent—Jesus the Christ. His agonizing death involves negativity and judgement—a passing over or becoming different by which an individual is rendered particular and finite. Yet the result of this death is not just the universality of living spirit, but the "unity" of universal and singular. This embodies the pattern of the first syllogistic figure in which a singular object of reference is the subject, a comprehensive universal is the predicate, and the middle term is a particular, or determinate concept. The movement from term to term is a simple becoming, transition, or passing over, the perishing of the finite individual into the universality of spirit. As an immediate transition, it incarnates the dynamic of the Barbara syllogism. An individual passes by way of particularity to being integrated with universality.

In the logic of syllogism the two aspects of form and content fall apart. The pattern of singular-particular-universal is indifferent to the dynamic of transition. Here, however, the particular is not simply a determinate concept—a third object of reference. It is rather a negative process of becoming, actualizing the negation that characterizes all determination. Indeed the agent—Christ—who initiates the process is the sensuous singular individual who is its presupposition. For he "places himself into judgement (*sich in das Urteil setzend*)." This self-introduced negativity transforms the universal substance into infinite subjectivity, for death here is not the final end, a limit in some sense external to the finite individual. It is the determination of his own activity—the dynamic of eternal, living, present spirit.

Natural religion venerates the dead; because the immediate transition of death has simply happened to the individual, he or she has not achieved subjectivity, but has become instead a mere shade. In contrast, revealed religion reflects on that transition in one particular instance; fundamental is the self-determining essence who eternally undergirds the universe and who is present both in the identity of the singular subject and in the universal spirit—identical in both the presupposition and the result. This identity is the self-differentiating agent that places himself in judgement and dies in absolute agony.

In revealed religion the content of this syllogism is simply presented to reflection as something external. It has not been produced by self-determining thought. It is *Vorstellung* and not *Begriff*. Incarnate in that content is the determining dynamic of comprehensive intelligence. However, its reflective form is still indifferent to its conceptual content.

IV

Revealed religion starts to become internalized in the second syllogism.

§570 2) This objective totality is the *inherent presupposition* for the *finite* immediacy of the singular subject, at first therefore something *other* for the subject and *intuited*, but the intuition of *inherent* truth; through this testimony of the spirit within it, it determines itself because of its immediate nature to be at first on its own vain and evil; further, according to the example of [the spirit's] truth and by means of faith in the unity *inherently* accomplished therein of the universal and the singular essentiality, it is also the movement of divesting itself of its immediate natural determination and of its will, and [the movement] of merging itself with that example and its inner nature in the agony of negativity, and so to know itself as united with the essence,...

In this second syllogism the mediating agent is a finite, singular subject, who presupposes the content of the first syllogism as something alien, even in its totality and generality. But in reflecting on that universal reality, singular subjects themselves are brought through a negative process of particularity: they find their particular nature, as distinguished from the universal, to be vain and evil. As a result this particularity merges with the universal truth of Christ's passion, now no longer intuited, but identified with their agony and negativity. Here is the form of the second figure: singularity synthesizing particularity and universality.

The mediating process this time is not a simple transition. The individual subjects dissociate themselves from their immediate contingent qualities to get at the essence, both of themselves and of universal reality. This self-negating act reproduces existentially the self-cancelling process of reflection.[4] Individuals think of themselves as external to the essence, even while they are determining what is essential.

The features reflection uses to determine what is essential not only characterize the process. They also constitute the subjects themselves. As a result, while differentiating themselves from the object of faith as vain and evil in contrast to the essential and good, the finite subjects discover that their very agony of self-negating subjectivity is identical with that rendered incarnate in the agonizing death pictured in the first syllogism. They discover a reflective analogy between their own experience of self-alienation and the self-determined death of the divine son.

As in the second figure[5] of the formal syllogism, the result is a particular judgement. Some singular subjects have experienced death to self and are subsumed into the universal spirit. But the process also embodies the reflective pattern of induction. For as one sinner's reflective experience is repeated by a number of others, making a finite set, it is extrapolated as a universal truth that extends to all finite spirit.

Within the logic of reflective inference, the synthetic act that brings together the terms in analogy, or the sample in induction, is external to the content of the syllogism. This discrepancy marks it as finite and to some extent contingent. However, in the experience of revealed religion, the self-reflexive act of self-cancelling is not simply an operation external to its subject. Rather the moment of self-alienation is the essential particularity by which finite subjects both distinguish themselves from, and find themselves one with, the universal essence—the presupposition of faith. This self-reflexive moment, when "he determines himself," thus becomes the central constituent in the dynamic of the inferential process, transcending the limitations of the formal logical structure. Yet it does not escape a moment of contingency. For the synthesis of the experience of self-alienation with the agonizing death of the incarnate one is an addition to the content of each, and not an implication of either. It is felt as a moment of experience, but not comprehended within the totality of thought.

V

In the first two syllogisms, Hegel provides us with enough clues to enable us to correlate them with the logic of inference. Much more cryptic is his characterization of the third.

> ...the essence, which 3) causes itself as indwelling in self-con-sciousness through this mediation and is the actual presence of spirit that is in and of itself as [it is the actual presence] of the universal.

In this case we must reconstruct the syllogism by extrapolating from the previous two. On the one hand it would be a syllogism of Hegel's third figure, in which universality mediates between singularity and particularity. This is suggested by the reference to spirit as the universal agent. On the other hand it would be an inference of necessity in which the middle term or operator determines the independent differences of the two extremes. Hegel's use of the reflexive form of *bewirken*—"causes itself"—would seem to support this inference.

One can, indeed, go further. The phrase, "causes itself as indwelling in self-consciousness," suggests a process of disjunction through which the universal particularizes itself into the various singular instances of self-alienation that embody the second syllogism. Its parallel, "is the actual presence of spirit," refers to the culminating ideal of the first syllogism, which is spirit now living and present in the world. The two clauses represent the two previous syllogisms and, although distinct from each other, they are incorporated into a both/and relation, one of the forms of a disjunctive judgement.

It is, however, no longer the idea of spirit, but *actual* spirit that is dynamically present. No longer is it contemplated as a presupposition for faith, but it is the reality of life being lived. The moment of negativity is not the simple transition of dying, nor is it the reflective identity of agonizing subjects. It is the process of disjunction itself—causing itself, indeed creating itself, through the individuated moments of negative experience and agonizing death. These are all incorporated into its comprehensive universality. Thus the disjunctive operation is not a subjective inference that requires reference to an objective whole to be complete. It transcends the finitude of conceptual thought by integrating syllogistic form and inferential process into a self-determining totality that requires no reference to anything external.

VI

Because spirit integrates the various moments of revealed religion into a comprehensive totality, it is able to leave behind the disjointed representations of doctrine and parable and express its truth in the conceptual language of philosophy.

§571 These three syllogisms, which constitute the *one* syllogism of the absolute mediation of spirit with itself are its revelation, which explicates its life in the cycle of concrete figures of representation. Out of their sundered occurrence and temporal and external succession the development of the mediation with their result, the locking together of spirit with itself, integrates itself not only to the simplicity of faith and of felt devotion but also to *thinking* within whose simplicity indeed the development achieves its breadth, but known as an indivisible interconnection of the universal, simple, and eternal spirit with itself. In this form of truth is truth the object of *philosophy*.

The third syllogism retains a moment of diversity. As the final stage it presupposes the two previous mediations of crucifixion and self-alienation. The three together embody the various aspects of the logic of syllogism. They reflect the three figures: S-P-U, P-S-U, S-U-P; they embody three types of inference—the simple transition of *Dasein*, the inductive and analogical syntheses of reflection, and the disjunctive self-determination of necessity. They characterize the three aspects of revealed religion: the transition from incarnation through crucifixion to the universal spirit is the moment of doctrine; reflection on that doctrine leads to conviction of sin and assurance of pardon, the moment of faith and personal devotion; comprehensive spirit convicts individuals of sin while integrating them into a universal fellowship, the moment of cult and community. In revealed religion these are represented as three distinct elements that fit uneasily together. For example, the moment of reflection leads towards an affirmation of personal responsibility and free will while the comprehensive moment supports a doctrine of predestination.

In the intuitive unity of faith and devotion, however, the three moments are felt to be not unrelated to each other. The first is a presupposition for the second; the third sets the other two within a comprehensive context. Together they somehow make up a single totality.

Hegel indicates this, for redemption and reconciliation is not simply a set of three syllogisms. "These three syllogisms," he says, "constitute the *one* syllogism of the absolute mediation of spirit with itself." Together they embody the moment of individuality or singularity.

Revealed religion provides some indication of the way this integration comes about. For in each of the three syllogisms the mediating agent is not a simple event, nor an externally introduced synthesis, but a *self-determining* operation. The individual existent who is one with the divine essence *places himself* into judgement—into a primordial division—in the agony of death. Through his own action he applies his own quality of finitude to himself. Finite spirits *condemn themselves* as evil when confronted with the story of the crucifixion. They self-reflexively identify their own essence. But both moments are initiated and completed through the *self-causation* of spirit comprehensive. It constrains the incarnate one as he moves towards his death; it convicts believers of their sin; and it does both as the self-causing, universal presence. It self-referentially determines itself.

Each of the three elements of doctrine, faith, and cult is thus a self-generating activity. But the agent is as yet different in each case. In the first, the agent is self-particularizing, in the second the agent is self-individuating, in the third, self-universalizing. From this perspective, however, they constitute the three moments of a single syllogism. Within this whole a simple transition or becoming leads from the historical given of doctrine's content through the existential agony of faith, in its finitude and alienation, to the comprehensive reality of the church; a reflective synthesis identifies the essential determination that integrates the particularity of each individual believer with the spirit of the crucified one; a comprehensive, self-determining operation generates in the cult the eternal recollection of the historical events which the spirit itself brought about and the perpetual conviction of sin that maintains the community. But these three operations are all part of one comprehensive dynamic in which disjunction generates both the transition and the reflection.

The reality of revealed religion is thus the singular, all-encompassing spirit that continually mediates itself through the transitions of faith and the reflection of devotion. Yet revealed religion does not characterize this reality as singular. Each syllogism is described with its own metaphors. They are assembled as a collection of discrete articles of faith that simply follow one another, leaving the impression that one can be omitted without damaging the others. The totality appears to be a contingent and arbitrary synthesis. The complex singularity inherent in three integrated syllogisms has not been expressed in its form. So the simplicity of the final moment will only become explicit when the manner of speaking that relies on temporal and external sequence is replaced by the conceptual structure of syllogism and inference. Then the inherent connections will become explicit and the diversity will be integrated into one totality. Such an achievement transcends the last remnant of relativity—of external relations and the mutual indifference of terms—and renders absolute and comprehensive the dynamic of spirit. In other words, Hegel's use of the language of judgement and syllogism does not belong to the sphere of revealed religion at all, but has already passed over into the comprehensive stage of philosophy.

VII

For Hegel the reasonableness of Christianity cannot be demonstrated by trying to discover a logical consistency between the assertions of doctrine. One must look rather at the content asserted. For that content describes processes that reproduce the inferences of thought and identifies moments that incarnate logical terms. This intrinsic rationality needs only to be made explicit and set in context by rational thought, self-referentially aware of its own operations. Revealed religion will then no longer lie outside the limits of reason; Christians will no longer face an ugly, broad ditch between rational truth and historical dogma; and the believer in miracles will no longer be conscious of a continuing miracle in his own spirit. For revealed religion will be the means by which an individual is integrated into the comprehensive dynamic of the universe, and rational philosophy will be the self-awareness that knows and comprehends that integration. The two are not in tension, but "are known as an indivisible interconnection of the universal, simple and eternal spirit with itself" (§571).

XIII

Is Hegel a Christian?

In his detective story, "The Man in the Passage," G.K. Chesterton sets the final scene in court. A number of witnesses had seen a figure in the passage that led to a murdered actress. Sir William Seymour saw a tall man, or at least "there was something about the thing that was not exactly a woman and yet was not quite a man; somehow the curves were different. And it had something that looked like long hair." Captain Cutler said it looked more like a beast, for "the brute has huge humped shoulders like a chimpanzee, and bristles sticking out of his head like a pig." Father Brown said, "the shape was short and thick, but had two sharp, black projections curved upwards on each side of the head or top, rather like horns."

The court was in confusion, but Father Brown calmly restored order. A panel had been slid across the passage, he suggested, and it had a looking glass on its face. Each witness, in describing what he thought was the murderer, had only been talking about himself.[1]

That is rather like what happens when people describe Hegel's philosophy. What is his ultimate religious commitment? Findlay calls him "the philosopher of liberal humanism."[2] Kaufmann represents him as saying: "In God I do not believe; spirit suffices for me."[3] And Roger Garaudy says: "Son Dieu est le Dieu-programme des humanistes et non le Dieu-personne des théologiens."[4]

Yet in contrast Lauer reports: "It is not strange that Hegel should see in the Christian revelation of the God-man a revelation just as much of what man is as of what God is."[5] And Claude Bruaire writes of the *Science of Logic*, "Non seulement cette *Logique* constitue l'assise conceptuelle du discours sur le Dieu révélé, non seulement elle lui fournit son organisation spéculative, mais elle prétend transcrire le Verbe éternel divin."[6]

141

We are as confused as those sitting in Chesterton's court room. And we rather suspect that the explanation is the same. Each writer sees in Hegel a version of his own image. To be sure, there are those who contrast their own position with Hegel's so that they can then offer a trenchant criticism. Merold Westphal accepts the humanist reading of a withering away of religion so that he can then offer a Christian response.[7] And Karl Marx rejects Hegel's Christianity so that he can establish his naturalism.[8]

Nonetheless the situation is confusing. And we crave for a Father Brown who will not only remind us that we have been using the mirrors of speculation and reflection all along, but will also help us to get at the real Hegel. It is, perhaps, presumptuous, but let me try to fill that rôle.

Our first question is one of criteria. How can we decide? For, as Hegel himself realized, our preconceptions of what makes sense and what is reasonable mold and constrain our interpretations of philosophy. If something is nonsense to us, then (we shall confidently assume) it must be nonsense to this obviously intelligent person we are studying. And if something has been profound and challenging in our intellectual history, we anticipate that any philosopher we respect will find it profound and challenging as well. It is because we bring our own presuppositions to the hermeneutical task that we discover in our author judgements and conclusions that are reasonably similar to our own. When we do not, we almost invariably caricature her or him in precisely those areas where we disagree.

Let us approach the question cautiously, then, and start from Hegel himself. He does not define religion in terms of doctrines or beliefs alone. Religion incorporates much more: it includes religious practice—the immediate sentiment of feeling and the public practice of cult. Feeling, cult, and doctrine make up the reality of religion.[9] Assessed against these three standards, where does Hegel stand with respect to Christianity?

I start with feeling. And I start at the very point from which the humanistic, atheistic interpretation draws its evidence: the feeling of the death of God. Let me cite, in my own translation, the passage from the *Phenomenology* in full:

The death of the mediator is the death not only of his *natural* side, that is, of his particular being-for-self. It is not only the dead shell from which the essence has already departed that dies, but the *abstraction* of the divine essence as well. For, in so far as his death has not yet completed the reconciliation, it is one-sided, knowing the simplicity of thought as the *essence* in contrast to reality. The extreme of the self has not yet achieved equal value with the essence; the self has this only in the spirit. The death of this representation contains, therefore, at the same time the death of the *abstraction of the divine being* which has not yet been posited as self. This is the agonizing feeling of the unhappy consciousness, that *God himself* has *died*. This hard expression is the expression of the most inner self-knowing in its simplicity, the return of consciousness into the depth of the night of I = I, which neither distinguishes nor knows anything outside of itself any longer. Hence this feeling is in fact the loss of *substance*—of its taking a position over against consciousness....[10]

The death of God as an abstract being; the return into isolation for the self; the self left alone to create its own world: these are the claims of humanism. And it is to this passage that Garaudy and others appeal when justifying their stance.

But we need to pause. For Hegel is not here talking about an intellectual liberation, a recognition that we are no longer slaves to an alien master, now free and independent in our own house.

He is talking about feeling—the feeling of an unhappy consciousness. And he describes it as agonizing: "schmerzliche." This is not a description of doctrine, but of lived experience.

As lived it is a moment in a process of becoming. And we should follow it through to its completion:

At the same time, however, this feeling is the pure *subjectivity* of substance—the pure certainty of itself—which is lacking in substance as object, as immediate or as pure essence. This knowing, therefore, is an inspiriting through which—its abstraction and lifelessness having died—substance has become subject; hence substance has become *actual*, a simple and universal self-consciousness.[11]

Here, it would seem, we have arrived at humanism. But humanists seldom report the range of experience here described. They do not talk of the agonizing feeling of the death of God, nor of the deep night of the lonely soul. They describe this movement in terms of exhilaration, of self-discovery. And if they do talk about the loss of faith in traumatic terms, they soon forget the trauma, and put it away as a part of their childish past.

But Hegel does not seem to do so. For he goes on in the next paragraph to stress the importance of movement—this movement through agonizing feeling to pure self-certainty. It is not simply as finished product, but also as process and transition that spirit is present. The movement retains all its moments, including the agonizing night of God's death. Only by dwelling within that total dynamic are spirit and community constituted.

The recurrent movement through dark night to simple self-certainty is not what I find in humanist religion, I must confess; nor do I find it in much Christianity. Evangelicals talk about the deep night of self-condemnation and the light of redemption. Liberals talk about finding oneself in love. Neither talk about the experience of the death of God.

Yet there are some who refer to an experience more profound and recognize that such an experience is not to be forgotten, but to be woven into the fabric of one's religious life. Indeed they talk about "the dark night of the soul." It is those wise in Christian mysticism who describe it.

Listen to Augustine Barker: "If the soul would elevate her spirit, she sees nothing but clouds and darkness. She seeks God, and cannot find the least marks or footsteps of His Presence; something there is that hinders her from executing the sinful suggestions within her, but what that is she knows not, for to her thinking she has no spirit at all, and, indeed, she is now in a region of all others most distant from spirit and spiritual operations—I mean, such as are perceptible."[12]

Or consider St. John of the Cross: "Under the stress of this oppression and weight, a man feels so much a stranger to being favored that he thinks, and so it is, that even that which previously upheld him *has ended* along with everything else, and that there is no one who will take pity on him."[13]

But that is not the end. For the moment of utter darkness is a transition to what Underhill calls the Unitive Life. "And later, when God judged that it was time, He rewarded the poor martyr for all his suffering. And he enjoyed peace of heart, and received in tranquillity and quietness many precious graces," writes Suso.[14]

St. John of the Cross adds: "It remains to be said, then, that even though this happy night darkens the spirit, it does so only to impart light concerning all things; and even though it humbles a person and reveals his miseries, it does so only to exalt him; and even though it impoverishes and empties him of all possessions and natural affection, it does so only that he may reach out divinely to the enjoyment of all earthly and heavenly things, with a general freedom of spirit in them all."[15]

Here in the confessions of great Christian mystics we discover the movement of experience that Hegel has described—through the deep night of a lonely soul into a simple and universal self-consciousness.

The lonely soul cannot find the least sign of God's presence; that which has previously upheld the proficient in religious faith has ended. But for Hegel this is not something transcendent, beyond time. Within the Lutheran tradition this experience of profound loss has been closely tied to the crucifixion. And Hegel's words echo those of Johann Rist's hymn: "O grosse Not! Gott selbst liegt tot. Am Kreuz ist er gestorben." God himself has died. Yet that loss is not dismissed into the irrelevant past in the manner of the humanists; it is retained and incorporated into a more profound experience of the spirit of God: "hat dadurch das Himmelreich uns aus Lieb erworben."[16]

The parallel is striking. Indeed the very language Hegel uses suggests the comparison: "The agonizing feeling that God himself has died...the return of consciousness into the depth of the night of I = I.... This knowing is an inspiriting through which, its abstraction and lifelessness having died, substance has become subject."

Does it tell us anything about Hegel? I think it does. For the fact that he can describe the whole experience and that he can recognize its importance as a complete movement, suggests that he is not talking about something alien. All too often, those who have not plumbed the depths dismiss and ignore this experience. Even if it is part of their past, they do not recognise its significance. They abandon themselves to the exhilarating freedom of the humanist or the confident assurance of the saved. The fact that Hegel places it only three pages before he starts talking about absolute knowing, however, suggests it is not something to be forgotten, relegated to the early obscurity of unhappy consciousness or the transient irrelevance of faith. And the fact that he describes it so accurately suggests that it is not simply something heard about, but something he himself has felt.

I conclude, then, that within Hegel's experience is to be found the profound religious feeling that only a few of the mystics talk about: the movement through the dark night of the soul into the unitive life. Such an experience, for all that it has found its echo in other traditions, is distinctively Christian, for it is intimately tied to the "one-sided representation of the death of the mediator" as its counter-part and completion.

Let me turn to the second criterion: the question of cult.

The chapter on Absolute Knowing in the *Phenomenology* integrates two moments out of the preceding discussion: the inherence of truth expressed in revealed religion, and truth on its own account as captured in the dynamic of the beautiful soul. Feeling has picked up the first of these; I now turn to the beautiful soul.

The important point here, once again, is the movement—the total picture. It starts with a moment of purity. "All life, and everything

spiritually essential has returned into this self and has lost its distinctness from the I. Hence the moments of consciousness are these
extreme abstractions, none of which stand firm, but rather each loses
itself in an other, and produces it."[17] Once again Hegel reminds us of
the unhappy consciousness.

But the beautiful soul cannot stay in this purity of self-knowing; it
must act and make itself actual. Any such action, however, is singular—the product of whim. What was intended as a way of actualizing
the good turns out to be evil. And the soul, no longer beautiful, comes
under severe judgement. For the other half of the beautiful soul—that
which in its self-knowing knows the good—contemptuously condemns the hypocrisy which intends the good and does the evil. Once
the acting and the judging have both found firm and independent
expression, a new moment appears. The one who acts confesses: "I
am evil"; the one who judges becomes more fixed in condemning and
repelling, driving the evil one to the point of madness. At the moment
where no hope seems possible the one who judges recognizes in the
agent his or her own action—that judging is also an act involving singularity and whim. The result is reconciliation.

Fear and trembling of a soul fully conscious of itself; action that
inevitably converts into evil; harsh and severe condemnation; forgiveness and reconciliation: these are the moments of the beautiful soul.
The claim to certainty at this stage involves the whole pattern starting
with pure intention, not just the final moment of reconciliation; this
total movement is taken up into absolute knowing.

It is tempting to think of this as the culmination of secular
humanity; today we might think of how the self-knowledge provided
by psychology and psychoanalysis leads to wisdom. Many have
looked for the prototype of this figure in the writings of Novalis, or in
the hero of romantic sensibilities. But there is something missing.[18]
For the modern approach to therapy dissolves the moment of condemnation, and the romantic ideal dissolves the moment of action.
One acts without judging; the other judges without acting; and so
there is no genuine forgiveness—no real reconciliation. Hegel requires
more. For the dynamic of the beautiful soul is a movement that must
continue to be repeated for the result to be reconfirmed. And the pure
self-knowledge of modern secularism in which "tout comprendre
c'est tout pardonner" forgets the process while exploiting the product.

This movement must continue to be reenacted; repeated reenact-
ment requires the institutions of a community—a community in
which rituals maintain action, judgement, and reconciliation as distinct moments. Hegel makes this clear at the point where, introducing

the discussion of the beautiful soul, he differentiates it from conscience.

> [Conscience] is that character of moral genius which knows
> the inner voice of its immediate knowledge to be the divine
> voice, and since in this knowing it knows determinate being
> in an equally immediate way, it is the divine creative power
> which has living force in its concept. It is, thereby, divine
> worship in itself, for its acting is the intuiting of its own
> divinity.[19]

That would seem to be enough; it talks about pure self-knowledge. One wonders why Hegel has to go on to the beautiful soul,
since the romantic ideal intuits its own divinity in its action. The next
sentence, however, provides an answer.

> This solitary worship is, at the same time, essentially the wor-
> ship of a *community*, and the pure inner self-*knowing* and self-
> perceiving goes on to become a moment of *consciousness*.

And the paragraph ends:

> As intuited knowing or knowing that has a being, religion is
> the speaking of the community concerning its spirit.[20]

The process must become objective within a community so that it can
be perceived and understood; this communal process involving
speech is the work of religion.

By placing this paragraph at the point of transition, Hegel distinguishes the dynamic of the beautiful soul from that of conscience as
the divine service of a community in contrast to the worship of a singular soul. He is stressing the importance of cult.

Once we investigate, we find the pattern of action, condemnation,
confession, and forgiveness captured in the practice of Lutheran confession. Listen to Luther's Small Catechism:

> What is confession? Confession consists of two parts. One is
> that we confess our sins. The other is that we receive absolu-
> tion or forgiveness from the confessor as from God himself....
> What sins should we confess?... Before the confessor we
> should confess only those sins of which we have knowledge
> and which trouble us. What are such sins? Reflect on your
> condition in the light of the Ten Commandments.[21]

The reference to the Ten Commandments recalls an earlier part of the Catechism which ends thus:

> God threatens to punish all who transgress these command-ments. We should therefore fear his wrath and not disobey these commandments. On the other hand, he promises grace and every blessing to all who keep them. We should therefore love him, trust in him, and cheerfully do what he has com-manded.[22]

Luther then offers a brief form for confession that ends:

> Then the confessor shall say: "God be merciful to you and strengthen your faith. Amen." Again he shall say: "Do you believe that the forgiveness I declare is the forgiveness of God?" Answer: "Yes I do." Then he shall say: "Be it done for you as you have believed. According to the command of our Lord Jesus Christ, I forgive you your sins in the name of the Father and of the Son and of the Holy Spirit. Amen. Go in peace."[23]

Lutheranism, unlike the other reforming churches, did not abol-ish personal confession. As the Augsburg Confession says: "The cus-tom has been retained among us of not administering the sacrament to those who have not previously been examined and absolved."[24] This is a central part of its cultic practice. And it is this act of divine worship on the part of the community that Hegel has analyzed and described in the beautiful soul. For it is this act which continually reenacts the movement from purity through action and judgement to forgiveness as a single movement to be maintained.

Absolute knowing presupposes not only the profound Christian feeling of the dark night of the soul, but also the cultic practice retained in the Lutheran churches of individual confession. By enshrining both as movements to be continually rehearsed, Hegel established himself securely within the Christian, indeed the Luther-an Christian, tradition.

But what about the third moment, the area of doctrine? Could Hegel be called orthodox? Did he believe the elements of Christian doctrine?

Although we could turn once again to the *Phenomenology* to answer this question, I shall refer instead to the chapter on revealed religion in the *Encyclopedia*.[25] Here Hegel describes Christian doctrine: an eternal creator who begets a son yet is spirit; the creation of heaven and earth, and the independence of evil, or fallen, finite beings; God and man immediately identified in a singular being who dies and thereby becomes universally present; fallen individuals who, in recognizing their own wickedness discover that they then share the life of God; and the continued mediation of this process within the community. Here are the basic ingredients of Christian doctrine. If Hegel collapses Easter and Pentecost into one event, talking not about a risen body, but a universal spiritual presence, he has good warrant. For the Gospel of John unites the two in a single incident. In Jesus' first appearance to his disciples, on the evening of Easter, he not only showed his hands and sides, but also "breathed on them, and said to them, 'Receive the Holy Spirit'."[26]

Is this, however, simply an account of what is reported in the tradition, a recognition that Hegel comes at the end of the Christian era, and so must take account of it, even though he has already moved beyond? I do not think so. For by the second edition of the *Encyclopedia* he makes explicit what previously was only implicit: the whole doctrinal statement has a logical structure. God before creation is self-determining universality; the created and fallen world is particularity; reconciliation is singularity. But the pattern extends even further. The eternal trinity itself involves the pattern of conceiving: universal, particular, and singular. Creation and fall reproduce the structures of judging: quality, quantity, relation, and modality. And, as I have shown elsewhere,[27] reconciliation embodies the network of three syllogisms.

To be sure, Christian doctrine is not expressed in such logical terms. It needs to be conceived philosophically before the inherent pattern is visible. But the relation is not one-sided. For philosophy also benefits from this encounter. Were it not for the fact that Christian doctrine represents as true of the cosmic order the same pattern that emerged in the processes of pure thought, Hegel could not have assumed that what is rational is actual and what is actual is rational.

Certainly the rational pattern is instantiated elsewhere. It is inherent in the whole experiential development described in the *Phenomenology*; it serves to explicate and organize the discoveries of the natural and human sciences into a coherent whole. But all of this could be, as Nietzsche puts it, "that kind of error without which a certain species of living being cannot exist."[28] Only with the affirmation that ultimate reality involves the pattern of creator and creation, fall and reconciliation, can Hegel establish his claim that reason and actuality are one. He must believe Christian doctrine; else his philosophy becomes illusion—nothing but a Kantian categorial framework which says nothing about the world in itself.

Let us take stock of where we are: Hegel gives evidence of an experiential awareness of Christian mysticism; he makes the cultic practice of individual confession constitutive of absolute knowing; his belief in Christian doctrine is a necessary condition for the truth of philosophy. In each area he betrays the distinctive traits that define the mainstream of the Christian tradition. We can therefore conclude that Hegel *was* a Christian.

For many, that would be enough to answer our initial question. For they claim that Hegel did not simply describe a process of absolute knowing, but also a state of absolute knowledge. If it is the latter he intended, then nothing that has happened since could affect his conclusion. The basic grammar of thought has been fixed, and Hegel would perforce continue to be Christian to the present day.

For some of us, however, that conclusion is not possible. As I have argued elsewhere,[29] there is strong evidence to suggest that Hegel saw even his own system as a culminating act of understanding, one that marked the beginning of a new dialectical transition into something other. If Hegel is genuinely open to the novelties and contingencies of history, then he cannot simply rest on his laurels and bask in his achievement. He must take account of *die Sache selbst:* what has actually occurred in the century and a half since his death. When we ask: "*Is* Hegel a Christian?" we have to confront the events of that hundred and fifty years to see whether Hegel's reponse would be the same now.

I must confess that I do not see anything really damaging in the atheism and humanism of Hegel's left-wing followers. When one has followed Hegel's exploration of the depths of religious experience, the traumas of confession and the subtle articulations of doctrine, the criticisms and challenges made by Feuerbach, Bauer, and Strauss seem banal and trivial. The real novelties are more significant.

I shall only suggest some, and they reflect my limited perspective. Nonetheless, it seems to me that they are worth taking seriously.

I have talked about the superficiality of humanism. But now even the dark night of the soul described by the mystics is in danger of becoming banal. For when we read the accounts of the gas chambers of Auschwitz, we see a faithful people who experienced the death of God—not as something confined to subjectivity, but as political events in an objective world. The diaries of the survivors and the trenchant stories of Elie Wiezel confront us with an experience of traumatic loss so radical that, even afterwards with the triumphant reestablishment of the state of Israel, it is hard to see the hand of God in those events.

Here is a dark night that surpasses all previous dark nights. And it has been built into the religious experience not of Christians, but of Jews.

In the fall of 1988, the war between Iran and Iraq stumbled to a close. Here, at least on the Iranian side, we find the action of convinced beautiful souls: radical condemnation and the judgement of evil. Yet even in the midst of the war that condemnation was converted to reconciliation.

> The 'conversion' of Iraqi PoWs during the war normally began from the moment of their capture. Revolutionary Guards and the Bassij volunteers would rush up to the cowering prisoners, embrace them, kiss them on the cheeks and welcome them as their Muslim brothers.[30]

Within a month of the end of the war Iran and Kuwait had reestablished diplomatic relations; two years later, Iran eagerly accepted Iraq's offer under constraint to make peace. In addition, throughout the darkest days of the conflict, Muslims from both sides put on the pilgrim white to pray side by side around the Kaaba in Mecca.

Here, too, is a process of action, judgement, and reconciliation. Once again it is not simply a ritual within a religious congregation. It is a movement of social and political entities; the structure of confession has acquired actuality in the realm of objective spirit. And once again it is not a Christian movement. Christianity has fallen apart into judgement without reconciliation, as in Ireland, or reconciliation without judgement, as in the ecumenical movement. It is Islam that has radicalized the movement of the beautiful soul, not Christianity.

It is not so easy to suggest where doctrine has gone. Certainly Christianity, confronted by the advances of modern science and the integrity of other religions, has been wont to surrender its claims to doctrinal truth and appeal to metaphor or nonrational insight. At the same time we have become aware of the sophisticated logics that the Indian tradition called Hinduism developed to articulate the nature of the world—a reliance on negation and the negation of negation that seems, to the uninitiated, to be far more subtle than that of Hegel. And we are only beginning to discover the rational discipline that found expression in the contradictions of Tao and the paradoxes of Zen. Here is religious doctrine that is not afraid to stretch what we mean by reason when articulating insight into truth. Once again it is not Christian, and once again, as we recall the nonviolence of Ghandi and watch the economic success of Japan, we find it embodied in a political and economic order.

Since 1830, the world has changed. It is passing through a process of becoming other and has dialectically converted into its opposite. But there is no single opposite. There are many. Jews, Muslims, Hindus, and Buddhists have all resurrected their religious faith and traditions from the limbo to which Hegel's philosophical history assigned them. But they are not only different from his Christianity. They are radically different from each other. Otherness seems to reign supreme.

According to Hegel, however, the dialectical production of otherness converts into speculation, the reflective unity of opposites. If we believe in his method, we should expect that out of the radical pluralism of the present there may yet develop a world community—one in which differences are maintained and deepened, even as people live together in mutual recognition. Once such a comprehensive community has become fully actualized, then philosophers will emerge to understand its structure and articulate its truth.

That truth will not be Christian, at least not the kind of Christianity that Hegel espoused. If it is Christianity, it will be Christianity sublated: preserved, but cancelled and transformed. However, the same thing will also be said about the many other traditions that in their own way have developed self-respect and presence. All will have an equal claim in the comprehensive picture that results.

I have no powers of prophecy. However, Hegel himself admits that only the method his system follows is true. These predictions have simply applied that method to some facets of our contemporary world: Hegel's philosophical understanding has passed over into its other; reflection will integrate that other with the reality out of which it sprang, producing a comprehensive totality; understanding will reemerge in that totality to understand its internal structure. In developing my prophecy in this way I am endeavoring to be faithful to Hegel. In other words, if Hegel could not easily be a Christian in our present day, he would at least believe in providence: that the method will work its inevitable way through history; that the actual will turn out to be rational.

There is, however, one final worry that calls this conclusion into question. Recall that the truth of the method—the pattern of dialectic, speculation, and understanding, of conceiving, judging, and inference—is finally established by the coherence between the content of Christian doctrine and the logic of rational thought. But we have suggested that Christian doctrine may no longer be the last and only word. And we have no idea what kind of doctrine will emerge in the distant future. Hegel's method itself, despite his confident assertion, may turn out to be partial and incomplete. If that were to happen, the foundations of his belief in providence itself would be shaken. And the last remnant of his Christianity could crumble. So our prophecy itself may be deception.

Is Hegel a Christian? The answer to that question we can now know only in part. For our knowledge is imperfect and our prophecy is imperfect. Once we become adults we shall put away such childish things. Nonetheless, as long as history continues there will abide some manner of doctrine, some kind of expectant experience and some sort of cultic community, however they find expression.[31]

NOTES

I. Lessing's Ditch

1. English translation in G. E. Lessing, *Theological Writings*, ed. H. Chadwick (London: A. and C. Black, 1956) 51–56.

2. Ibid. 53. Notice the parallel of this argument with that advanced by David Hume in his essay "On Miracles."

3. Ibid. 54.

4. See the title page of S. Kierkegaard, *Philosophical Fragments*, tr. D. F. Swenson (Princeton: Princeton University Press, 1957), iii: "Is an historical point of departure possible for an eternal consciousness; how can such a point of departure have any other than a mere historical interest; is it possible to base an eternal happiness upon historical knowledge?" and *Concluding Unscientific Postscript*, tr. D. F. Swenson & W. Lowrie (Princeton: Princeton University Press, 1953), 86, where there is a discussion of the claim "that the transition by which it is proposed to base an eternal truth upon historical testimony is a leap."

5. F. W. J. Schelling, *Sämmtliche Werke* (Stuttgart: Cotta, 1856–61) I.10:154, hereafter cited as *Werke*. Schelling had used the expression earlier in an aside during his "Lectures on the Method of Academic Studies" of 1802 (I.5:250).

6. "Contingent truths of historical fact and eternal truths of reason: the challenge of Lessing's 'ditch' and the responses of Hegel and Schelling." Diss. Toronto, 1970.

7. J. W. Burbidge, *On Hegel's Logic* (Atlantic Highlands, N.J.: Humanities, 1981), hereafter cited as *On Hegel's Logic..*

II. The First Chapter of Hegel's Larger Logic

1. C. Taylor, *Hegel* (Cambridge: Cambridge University Press, 1975) 233.

2. M. Theunissen, *Sein und Schein* (Frankfurt a/M: Suhrkamp, 1980) 191.

3. *HGW*, 21.18–19; *SL*, 40f.

4. M. Inwood, *Hegel* (London: Routledge, 1983) 310.

155

5. Burbidge, *On Hegel's Logic*, 42–5.

6. *HGW*, 11.7, 21.8; *SL*, 27–8

7. "He fails to follow [the principle that a philosopher is to be allowed to interpret himself] in insisting that Hegel's psychology explicates the ground that underlies and justifies the transitions, reflections and conceptualizations that constitute the *Logic*." (Alan White, *Graduate Faculty Philosophy Journal*, X [Winter 1985] 172.) "What is, perhaps, most consistently disconcerting is the author's insistence on viewing *thought* as the subjective activity of *thinking*." (Quentin Lauer, *International Philosophical Quarterly*, XXIII [March 1983] 96.) "It seems that, in the last analysis, Burbidge can only defend the starting point which he determines for Hegelian logic through psychology if he can show that it is made possible by the starting point for logic which Hegel determines through phenomenology." (Martin J. DeNys, *Man and World*, XVI [1983] 161.) "We are left with the suspicion, therefore, that Burbidge has been trying indeed to validate Hegel's logic on psychological grounds; and to the extent that this was his intention, he cannot escape the charge of psychologism." (George di Giovanni, *The Owl of Minerva*, XIV 1 [September, 1982] 4). See Burbidge, *On Hegel's Logic*, Chapter 2, pp 6–21, and in particular endnote 2 on page 234f which mentions evidence in Hegel that might support the approach taken.

8. I must say that I have looked for the arguments that Frege and Husserl use to support this claim, but without success. It appears to be a presupposition, rather than a theorem. The argument that follows is a reconstruction.

9. See *HGW*, 11.44, 21.69; *SL*, 82.

10. Burbidge, *On Hegel's Logic*, 22–34.

11. *HGW*, 21.69–70; *SL*, 82f.

12. I can recall the electric moment in class when, in discussing "With What Must a Science Begin" and the indeterminacy of pure being, a student erupted: "But that is simply nothing at all." That "intuitive" reaction is what Hegel attempts to describe in his obscure prose which, as Dieter Henrich points out in "Anfang und Methode der Logik" (*Hegel im Kontext* [Frankfurt a/M: Suhrkamp, 1971] 73–94), is cluttered with negative formulations that cancel the terminology of reflection. The language used to display the move of implication is more complicated than the move itself.

13. Note here that this appeal to positing and presupposing uses the language appropriate to positing reflection. The recall of a presupposition just at the point where thought has reached its contrary as an implication is a consistent theme of Hegel's analysis. See, for example, the third and fourth paragraphs of "The Essential and the Unessential" (*HGW*, 11.245; *SL*, 394f), and the first paragraph in 2. under "The Chemical Process" (*HGW*, 12.150; *SL*, 730).

14. *HGW*, 11.44, 21.70; *SL*, 83.

15. *HGW*, 11.7, 21.8; *SL*, 28.

16. See Chapter 4: "Where is the Place of Understanding?"

17. *HGW*, 11.56, 21.92; *SL*, 105f.

18. Recall that when Hegel reaches the culminating point in individuating the process of conceiving, he has generated the disjunctive syllogism.

19. *HGW*, 11.57, 21.93; *SL*, 106.

20. See *Enc.*, §§79–82.

21. *HGW*, 21.44; *SL*, 59.

22. *HGW*, 21.45; *SL*, 60.

III. Transition or Reflection

1. But see *Enc.* §81 (first edition §15), where dialectic takes its place with speculative reason and understanding as one of the "sides" of logical form.

2. *HGW*, 21.110; *SL*, 122.

3. *HGW*, 11.65

4. Some intermediate stages in the development from the first edition to the second are found in the different orders for the categories in the first and second editions of the *Encyclopedia of the Philosophical Sciences*.

5. Curious at first is this use of *posited* in characterizing the development *in itself*. One notes the distinction between the passive "*a* is posited with *b*" and the active "*a* posits *b*," and sees the parallel to "proceeds" and "elicits." The former in both pairs appears to be something that happens immediately, whereas the latter is determined reflectively.

6. *HGW*, 21.109–110; *SL*, 121–2.

7. It is the merit of D. Henrich's paper, "Anfang und Methode der Logik," in *Hegel im Kontext* (Frankfurt a/M: Suhrkamp, 1971) 73–94, that he draws this distinction clearly and uses it to explicate the beginning of the *Logic*.

8. *HGW*, 11.59. I should note that I am following a convention used in *On Hegel's Logic* where I translated the German word *Dasein* as "a being." See there footnote 19 on page 245.

9. *HGW*, 21.97; *SL*, 109.

10. M. Miller has demonstrated the importance of transition for Schleiermacher's philosophy of religion. See his *Der Uebergang, Schleiermachers Theologie des Reiches Gottes*, Ph.D. diss. theol. Heidelberg.

11. *HGW*, 11.44, 21.69; *SL*, 82–3. My italics.

12. See *Encyclopedia* §§446–450 and §§465–468, and my commentary on this section in *On Hegel's Logic* 6–21. Once one moves beyond the pure immediacy of 'being' and 'nothing' the pure immediacy of intuition is not an appropriate characterization of the operations of intelligence.

13. *HGW*, 21.104; *SL*, 116.

14. The development in "Something and Other" is more complicated than usual, suggesting that Hegel had not sufficiently worked through the implications of fitting the earlier material to this frame.

This will have to suffice as an explanation of the changes introduced into the second edition. What is required is a full-length study and double commentary of the whole book.

15. See Henrich, "Anfang und Methode der Logik."

16. *HGW*, 11.249; *SL*, 399. Reference should be made to several valuable commentaries on "Reflection:" D. Henrich, "Hegels Logik der Reflexion," in *Hegel im Kontext*, 95–156, and G. di Giovanni, "Reflection and Contradiction. A Commentary on some passages of Hegel's *Science of Logic*," *Hegel-Studien*, 1973, 131–161. By relating reflection more directly to immediate transitions, my interpretation differs from theirs. See *On Hegel's Logic*, 63–84.

17. Recall the final sentence in the quotation from *HGW*, 21.110 (*SL*, 122) above, which refers to positive/negative and cause/effect as each showing the other in itself.

18. See *HGW*, 11.15; *SL*, 43: "Logic, on the other hand, can presuppose none of these forms of reflection, or rules and laws of thinking, for they constitute a part of its content, and have to be first established within it." In identifying the three operations as functions of one reflection and not of different ones, my interpretation differs from those of Henrich and di Giovanni.

19. Here, then, I indicate my conviction that the external (*äussere*) reflection of the Doctrine of Essence is the same as the external (*äusserliche*) reflection of the preface to the first edition: "Since philosophy is to be a science, it cannot (as I have recalled elsewhere) borrow its method from any subordinate science, such as mathematics; as little as it can be satisfied with categorical assurances from inner intuition or make use of arbitrary reasoning on the basis of external reflection." (*HGW*, 11.7; *SL*, 27) As I shall subsequently show, the difference is not in the operation of reflection itself, but whether it occurs determined within the fundamental systematic integrity of conceptual thought, or whether it is an element of arbitrary reasoning (*Räsonnement*). While I here take issue with one element of his argument, may I pay tribute to W. Jaeschke's "Äusserliche Reflexion und immanente Reflexion," *Hegel-Studien*, Band 13, 85–117, which has performed a signal service in tracing the development of Hegel's use of Reflection.

20. See *HGW*, 21.110; *SL*, 122.

21. This is the proper reference for Sartre's distinction rather than the *Phenomenology*. For the *Phenomenology* distinguishes *an sich* from *für es*, not from *für sich*. Since French, like English, cannot so easily distinguish between the two latter phrases, Sartre has collapsed them into one, and made *pour soi* self-reflexive. But neither *für es* nor *für sich* is strictly self-reflexive. The former is simply a consciousness of something, and the latter is a German idiom: "We say that something is *für sich* to the extent that it overcomes the otherness, its relating and community with another, repels them and is abstracted from them. The other remains for it only *as* something overcome, as *its moment*. *Fürsichsein* consists in having gone beyond the limit—beyond its otherness—in such a way that, as this negation, it is the infinite *return* into itself" (*HGW*, 21.145; *SL*, 158). This idiom does not require reflection, and thus Hegel discusses *Fürsichsein* in the logic of being and not in essence.

22. See *HGW*, 12.11; *SL*, 577: "From this perspective *concept* is at first to be seen in general as *the third* to *being* and *essence*, to the *immediate* and to *reflection*. To that extent being and essence are the moments of its becoming. It is, however, their *foundation* and *truth*, as the identity within which they are swallowed up and contained."

23. Henrich, *Hegel im Kontext*, 98f.

24. *HGW*, 12.43; *SL*, 612.

25. *HGW*, 12.49; *SL*, 618–9: "What is negative in the universal, whereby this is something *particular*, has previously been determined as two-faced: to the extent that it faces *inwardly*, the particular remains a universal; in facing outwardly it is *determinate;* the return of this aspect into the universal is twofold: *either* through *abstraction*, which leaves the particular aside and ascends to a *higher*, indeed the *highest*, genus; *or* through *individuality*, to which the universal within the determinacy descends."

26. See *HGW*, 12.124–5; *SL*, 702: "The disjunctive syllogism is by and large in the determination of *universality*, its middle is the *A* as *genus* and as completely *determinate;* through this unity that previously inner content is now posited, and on the other hand its being posited, or the form, is not an external, negative unity over against an indifferent being, but now identical with that genuine content. The whole determination of the concept's form is posited in their determinate difference and at the same time in the simple identity of the concept."

27. *HGW*, 12.32; *SL*, 600: "The capacity to conceive in general has customarily been expressed by 'understanding'." *Ibid.* 12.41; 610: "Further, it is to be considered as the infinite force of understanding that it separates the concrete into abstract determination, and grasps that depth of the difference which alone has the power of effecting its own demise." See Chapter 4.

28. Because the comprehensive totality of conceptual thought is self-determining, Hegel withdrew that predicate from the immediate category "a

being" when revising the *Logic*. For, "in the sphere of Being the *self-determining* of the concept is only *in itself,* and so it is called a transition." (*HGW,* 21.110; *SL,* 122)

29. *HGW,* 21.110; *SL,* 122.

30. For example, Hegel "has found only the *abstract, logical, speculative* expression for the movement of history, which is not yet the *actual* history of mankind as a presupposed subject, but only the *act of procreation,* the *genetic history* of mankind." "Ökonomische-philosophische Manuskripte (1844)" in *Marx-Engels Werke,* Ergänzungsband, Erster Teil (Berlin: Dietz, 1968) 570.

31. See the second *Thesis on Feuerbach:* "It is in Praxis that man must prove the truth, that is, prove the actuality and power, the this-sidedness of his thinking." *Marx-Engels Werke,* Band III (1969) 533.

32. *HGW,* 11.25, 21.38; *SL,* 54.

IV. Where is the Place of Understanding?

1. J. N. Findlay, *Hegel, A Re-examination* (London: Allen and Unwin; New York: Humanities, 1958) 62.

2. E. E. Harris, *An Interpretation of the Logic of Hegel* (Lanham, Md.: University Press of America, 1983) 40.

3. M. Westphal, "Hegel's Theory of the Concept," in *Art and Logic in Hegel's Philosophy,* ed. W. E. Steinkraus & K. L. Schmitz (Atlantic Highlands, N.J.: Humanities, 1980) 108.

4. *Enc.* §80, Addition; *The Logic of Hegel,* tr. W. Wallace (Oxford: Clarendon, 1892) (henceforth Wallace) 144.

5. *HGW,* 9.27; *Phen.,* 18.

6. *HGW,* 9.27; *Phen.,* 19.

7. *Enc.* §79; Wallace, 143. In German: "*Näherer Begriff und Einteilung der Logik.*"

8. *Enc.* §80; Wallace, 143.

9. *Enc.* §81; Wallace, 147.

10. *Enc.* §82; Wallace, 152.

11. Harris, *Interpretation,* 227.

12. Findlay, *Hegel,* 222, 223.

13. *Enc.* §80, Addition; Wallace, 144, 145.

14. *HGW*, 12.39; *SL*, 607.

15. *Hegel's Science of Logic*, tr. W. H. Johnston & J. G. Struthers (London: Allen & Unwin; New York: Macmillan, 1929) II, 241f.

16. It is interesting that Miller does not italicize understanding when it first appears in Hegel's text (*HGW*, 12.40; *SL*, 609), although Hegel uses *Sperrdruck*, the German device of spacing the letters of a word when it is to be stressed.

17. *HGW*, 12.41; *SL*, 610.

18. *HGW*, 12.42; *SL*, 611.

19. *HGW*, 12.42f; *SL*, 611f.

20. It is in the section "The Singular" that Hegel identifies the abstract universal. As the antithesis of the singular, it must yet be combined with it. This finds expression in the positive judgement: "The singular is the (abstract) universal."

21. An earlier statement of the point may be found in Burbidge, *On Hegel's Logic* 220ff. While I had already been forced to notice that Hegel placed his discussion of understanding in the third book of the *Logic*, at the time I had not yet fully worked out its implications.

22. *HGW*, 12.32; *SL*, 600.

23. See *On Hegel's Logic*, Chapters 13 and 14.

24. *HGW*, 21.38; *SL*, 54.

25. See Chapter 2: "Transition or Reflection."

26. When one considers the significant changes that the Chapter on *Dasein* went through between the first edition of the *Logic* in 1812 and the second edition in 1831, with three intermediate versions varying in concepts and order, summarized in the three editions of the *Encyclopaedia*, it seems that Hegel sees the categorial framework of the logic itself as detail that will continue to be elaborated.

27. See Zimmerli's paper, "Is Hegel's *Logic* a Logic?" in *Hegel and his Critics* (Albany: SUNY Press, 1989) 191–202.

V. The Necessity of Contingency

1. D. Henrich, "Hegels Theorie über den Zufall," *Kantstudien*, 50 (1958–9) 135; reprinted in *Hegel im Kontext* (Frankfurt a/M: Suhrkamp) 164 n8.

2. *HGW*, 11.21, 21.34; *SL*, 50.

3. *Enc.* §19.

4. See in the remark to *Enc.* §20, where Hegel distinguishes "representing" from "understanding" in that understanding posits relationships such as universal/particular and cause/effect in their necessary connection, whereas representations simply put terms next to each other with an "also." See as well the discussion in Chapter 1.

5. See *Enc*, §§79–82.

6. *HGW*, 11.383–4; *SL*, 545. In my translation I assume the parallelism of the two subordinate clauses, so that *ebensosehr* repeats *als möglich bestimmt*.

7. In the *exposition de texte* that follows, the note at the end of each paragraph will cite the appropriate page and line numbers from *Hegels Gesammelte Werke*, but only the page number from Miller's *Science of Logic*.

8. *HGW*, 11.381:29–35; *SL*, 542.

9. *HGW*, 11.382:1–3; *SL*, 542–3.

10. *HGW*, 11.382:4–11; *SL*, 543.

11. *HGW*, 11.382:12–20; *SL*, 543.

12. *HGW*, 11.382:21–383:14; *SL*, 543–4.

13. *HGW*, 11.383:15–18; *SL*, 544.

14. *HGW*, 11.383:19–28; *SL*, 544.

15. *HGW*, 11.383:29–35; *SL*, 544.

16. *HGW*, 11.383:36–384:6; *SL*, 545.

17. *HGW*, 11.384:7–12; *SL*, 545.

18. *HGW*, 11.384:13–16; *SL*, 545.

19. *HGW*, 11.384:17–18; *SL*, 545.

20. The four stages are 'actuality' and 'possibility', each considered as grounded and as groundless.

21. *HGW*, 11.384:19–30; *SL*, 545.

22. *HGW*, 11.384:31–34; *SL*, 545.

23. *HGW*, 11.384:35–385:12; *SL*, 545–6.

24. *HGW*, 11.385:18–29; *SL*, 546.

25. *HGW*, 11.385.30–386:9; *SL*, 546–7.

26. *HGW*, 11.386:10–22; *SL*, 547.

27. *HGW*, 11.386:23–37; *SL*, 547.

28. *HGW*, 11.387:1–22; *SL*, 547–8.

29. *HGW*, 11.387:23–388:5; *SL*, 548–9.

30. *HGW*, 11.388:6–20; *SL*, 549.

31. *HGW*, 11.388.21–389:7; *SL*, 549–550.

32. *HGW*, 11.389:8–16; *SL*, 550.

33. *HGW*, 11.389:17–18; *SL*, 550.

34. *HGW*, 11.389:21–30; *SL*, 550.

35. *HGW*, 11.389:31–390:2; *SL*, 550–1.

36. *HGW*, 11.390:3–15; *SL*, 551.

37. *HGW*, 11.390:16–28; *SL*, 551.

38. *HGW*, 11.390:29–391:4; *SL*, 551–2. See also *HGW*, 11.391:25–39; *SL*, 552–3.

VI. Challenge to Hegel

1. Schelling, *Werke* I.10:154, 213. See "On the Proof of the Spirit and of Power," in G. E. Lessing, *Theological Writings*, tr. & ed. H. Chadwick (London: A & C Black,1956) 55.

2. These were published in the four volumes of the second *Abtheilung* of the *Werke*. All translations from Schelling are my own.

3. Among works on the *Logic* in English not already cited are W. Wallace, *Prolegomena to the Study of Hegel's Philosophy and Especially of his Logic* (Oxford: Clarendon, 1894); J. B. Baillie, *The Origin and Significance of Hegel's Logic* (London: Macmillan, 1901); J. M. E. McTaggart, *A Commentary on Hegel's Logic* (Cambridge: Cambridge University Press, 1910); G. R. G. Mure, *A Study of Hegel's Logic* (Oxford: Clarendon, 1950); M. Rosen, *Hegel's Dialectic and its Criticism* (Cambridge: Cambridge University Press, 1982); and T. Pinkard, *Hegel's Dialectic: The Explanation of Possibility* (Philadelphia: Temple University Press, 1988).

4. J. G. Fichte, *Science of Knowledge*, tr. P. Heath & J. Lachs (New York: Appleton Century Croft, 1970).

5. See *Werke*, II.1:297.

6. See *Werke*, II.1:304: "*Those* possibilities, however, which can be thought not simply in the others, but, *qua* what is, cannot at all *not* be thought

(for take away what is, then also all thought is taken away); those possibilities, therefore, which are not simply what are to be thought, but are what are not at all not to be thought, are hence thought necessarily (—thus in their way and in the realm of reason *are* just as much as the actualities of experience are in *their* realm): those possibilities are what are first and those from which all others are derived—those, therefore, which as far as possible for us turn into principles of all being."

7. *Werke*, II.1:326. This need to *experience* what happens when one thinks serves to link this rational procedure to induction: "As there are two types of induction, so there is also a twofold experience. The one says what is actual and what is not actual; this is what is commonly so called. The other says what is possible and what impossible; this is acquired in thinking.... Thinking is therefore experience as well."

8. See *Werke*, II.1:300: "For if it is principles, hence what is most universal, that is sought for in the face [of the incapacity], then this [fact], even if it is purely psychological, comes under consideration precisely *not* as such, but in terms of its universal and objective side. Taken not subjectively, but examined in terms of its constitutive principles, the psychological fact will, with respect to objective import, yield place to no other."

9. "*Mē on = dynamei on.*" Schelling refers to Aristotle, *Metaphysics*, IV,4: *Werke*, II.1:288f.

10. Such is the idealist's reworking of Descartes' argument regarding the *cogito*. 'What can be' replaces the 'I' because the 'I' involves an empirical content and a contrast with the 'non-I', which suggests that it is not strictly universal but limited. When thought abstracts from the 'I-ness' of the 'I', only the pure possibility of being remains. Schelling calls *das Seinkönnende* pure subjectivity.

11. It might be possible to interpret this contrast in symbolic terms. 'What can be,' as the negative of 'what is' could be symbolized as $-A$. By addition one can augment this to include its contrary: $--A$ (or A). When reason tries to conjoin these two ($-A$ & $--A$) it discovers that the conjunction cannot be thought. Therefore reason must negate it through a conditional negation: $-(-A$ & $--A)$. This is equivalent to A v $-A$ (by De Morgan's theorem)—in Boolean algebra the addition of the two in which neither remains pure in its isolation.

12. I. Kant, *Critique of Judgement*, tr. J. H. Bernard (New York: Hafner, 1951) §76. Compare here Schelling's own statement, *Werke*, II.3:58f: "*What* exists, or more precisely, what will exist...—this is what the rational science is about; this may be apprehended a priori. But *that* it exists does not follow at all; for nothing at all could exist. That anything at all exists and that in particular this particular thing apprehended a priori exists in the world can never be affirmed by reason without experience."

13. This is the problem taken up by Kant in the "Transcendental Deduction" of his *Critique of Pure Reason*.

14. *Werke*, II.3:62.

15. *Werke*, II.1:388. The Greek word (*existamenon*) is a passive participle of the verb form from which is derived the noun form 'ecstasy'.

16. "The rational science cannot demonstrate in experience the final Idea (which is indeed the content of reason that remains situated *within* reason) in the way [it has demonstrated] all the other ideas that have come to pass in it; and yet just *this* concept has the peculiarity of being the one that does not remain indifferent to the actual existence of what is claimed therein, in the way it was, in relation to all the preceding, a matter of indifference to the philosophizing subject whether it existed." *Werke*, II.3:171.

17. *Werke*, II.3:7.

18. *Werke*, II.1:464.

19. Ibid.

20. Ibid.

21. It may appear as if the negative philosophy is a necessary condition for the positive—as if reason had to follow the pathway of despair before it would surrender itself to ecstasy. But Schelling would not agree: "The positive philosophy is what is always and originally willed, but because it was mistaken, or followed down a false path, it called for the criticism out of which the negative philosophy then proceeded in the way I have shown—[a philosophy] which has its value and significance only *as* negative, that is to the extent that it does not will to be positive itself, but posits the positive outside itself." *Werke*, II.3:153.

22. The phrase *nothing prevents* recurs frequently in Schelling's text. See, for example, *Werke*, II.3:264, 4:338.

23. *Werke*, II.3:129.

24. A comparison with C. S. Peirce's logic of abduction is instructive. Like the method *per posterius*, abduction or hypothesis proposes a middle term that connects the universals of common knowledge with the particulars of an individual case. There is, however, an indefinite range of possible middle terms, not just one reflectively established. And the givens of experience are ambiguous; they do not divide themselves into essential and accidental qualities. Lacking inevitability, the crucial inferential move becomes an inspired guess. On the logic of Peirce's abduction, see my "Peirce on Historical Explanation," in *Pragmatism and Purpose: Essays presented to T. A. Goudge*, ed. Sumner *et al.* (Toronto: University of Toronto Press, 1981), 15–27. Peirce mentions the influence of Schelling in *Collected Poems of Charles Sanders Peirce*, ed. C. Hartshorne and P. Weiss (Cambridge, Mass.: Harvard University Press, 1934) 6.102.

25. The statements concerning Hegel in this paragraph receive justification elsewhere in this volume. See in particular Chapter 3: "Transition or

Reflection"; Chapter 5: "The Necessity of Contingency"; and Chapter 7: "Is Hegel a Rationalist or an Empiricist?"

26. In response to Schelling's appeal to the ultimacy of will, Kierkegaard rejects will as well as reason as a basis for faith, "for all human volition has its capacity within the scope of an underlying condition." *Philosophical Fragments* 50. Thus, despite a common interpretation, Kierkegaard's leap of faith is not an act of will, but something even will finds impossible.

VII. Is Hegel a Rationalist or an Empiricist?

1. . *GPR*, 14; *Hegel's Philosophy of Right*, tr. T. M. Knox (Oxford: Clarendon, 1942) 10.

2. K. Popper, *The Open Society and its Enemies*, Vol II: *The High Tide of Prophecy: Hegel, Marx and the Aftermath* (London: Routledge & Kegan Paul, 1966) 40.

3. *HGW*, 19.187n; *Enc.* §250.

VIII. Concept and Time in Hegel

1. "But we know that for Hegel, Time *is* the Concept." "Hegel is the first to identify the Concept and Time." Alexander Kojève, *Introduction to the Reading of Hegel*, ed. A. Bloom (New York & London: Basic Books, 1969) 154, 131. French original: *Introduction à la lecture de Hegel* (Paris: Gallimard, 1947) 431, 365 (From now on the French reference will precede that of the English translation [ET].) Philip Grier, in "The End of History and the Return of History," *The Owl of Minerva*, XXI, 2 (1990) 131–144, points out that Kojève derived this interpretation from Koyré.

2. My translation. *HGW*, 9.429: "Die *Zeit* ist der Begriff selbst der *da ist.*" *Phen.*, 487: "Time is the Notion itself that *is there.*"

3. *HGW*, 9.429; *Phen.*, 487.

4. Kojève, *Introduction*, 338; ET, 102.

5. Kojève, *Introduction*, 380; ET, 149.

6. Another puzzling comment of Kojève's fails to do justice to this fact. Referring to the last two paragraphs of the *Phenomenology* he claims that Hegel identifies nature with space and time with history (Kojève, *Introduction*, 366; ET, 133). This can happen only through a very perverse reading of the text. Hegel writes: "This sacrifice is the renunciation in which spirit sets forth its own becoming in the form of *free, contingent happening,* intuiting its pure *self* as *time*, external to it; and also its *being* as space. This its final becoming—

Nature—is its living immediate becoming...." (*HGW*, 9.433; *Phen.*, 492) If nature is a *Werden*, or becoming, it cannot be simply identified with space, but is essentially temporal.

7. See Chapter 2 above.

8. See *Enc.* §§86–88; also the *Science of Logic*, Book I, Section I, Chapter I.

9. *Enc.* §258 as well as its Addition from the lecture material.

10. This embodies the process which Hegel calls 'bad infinity' in contrast to the 'valid infinite' of the circle. See *Enc.* §94 and §95, and *Science of Logic*, *HGW*, 21.126–137; *SL*, 137–150.

11. Compare the difficulties Kojève has with this relation: "(If the opposition of Life and Spirit exists), Life is not historical; therefore there is no biological dialectic; therefore there is no conceptual understanding of life.... Hence (Hegel's) absurd philosophy of Nature...." (Kojève, *Introduction*, 378; ET 146). Because Kojève identifies the Concept with Time, he can only use 'time' in the sense of historical time—that temporal process which has conceptual meaning. Therefore he cannot make sense of a dialectical comprehension of natural structures.

12. See *HGW*, 9.429; *Phen.*, 487.

13. See *Enc.* §259, Addition from the lectures: "In nature, where time is *now*, there never develops a subsisting differentiation of those dimensions (past, present and future); they are necessary only in subjective representation, in memory and in fear or hope."

14. The dialectic of this process is carefully presented by Hegel in the section on sense certainty in the *Phenomenology*, *HGW*, 9.67–8; *Phen.*, 63–4.

15. This is an important concept in Hegel, noted particularly by E. L. Fackenheim in his *The Religious Dimension of Hegel's Thought* (Bloomington: Indiana University Press, 1967) 98.

16. See *Enc.* §§452–4.

17. See *GPR* §3, Remark.

18. This is stressed by Hegel in his preface to the *Philosophy of Right*. This discussion of the future is based on *Enc.* §§469–552 and *GPR* §§4–29. Reference should also be made to the *Philosophy of Right* and the *Lectures on the Philosophy of History*.

19. There is an interesting difference in Hegel's German between the two, however. The *Phenomenology* uses the present participle: "Die offenbare Religion"; the *Encyclopaedia* uses the past: "Die geoffenbarte Religion." Both, however, are analyses of Christianity.

20. This discussion is based on *Enc.* §§569–571. Chapter 12 below offers a

more detailed exposition of this passage. The analysis is not inconsistent with the description of revealed religion in the *Phenomenology*.

21. All from *Phenomenology: HGW*, 9.429; *Phen.*, 487. Note that the philosopher's awareness of sharing the absolute's life is a necessary condition for justifying his claim that the *speculative* move in logic (that which recognizes the circularity of dialectical thought) is sound.

22. *Science of Logic: HGW*, 21.60:29; *SL*, 74.

IX. The Inequity of Equality

1. *Sämtliche Werke*, 20.517; tr. Z. A. Pelczinski and T. M. Knox, *Hegel's Political Writings* (Oxford: Clarendon, 1964) 329–30.

2. G. W. F. Hegel, *Schriften zur Politik und Rechtsphilosophie*, ed. G. Lasson (Hamburg: Meiner, 1923) 442; tr. H. S. Harris and T. M. Knox (Albany: SUNY Press, 1979) 125.

3. *HGW*, 9.260–264; *Phen.*, 290–294.

4. See *HGW*, 9.316–323; *Phen.*, 355–363.

5. The texts on the logic translate the German "*Gleichheit*" as "likeness," but it is also the term used for "equality."

6. See *HGW*, 11.267–270; *SL*, 418–421.

7. See J. D'Hondt, *Hegel In His Time* (Peterborough: Broadview, 1988).

8. *HGW*, 11.272–290; *SL*, 424–443.

9. *HGW*, 9.109–110; *Phen.*, 111–112. I have used different genders for the pronouns to keep the two individuals distinct in the description. It is a matter of indifference which gender is used where, or indeed whether the same gender is used for both participants.

10. See *Enc.* §534; *GPR* §§250–256. What he would say about the modern corporation which, in its turn, abstracts a particular economic interest from the total life of the individuals that make it up is something about which we can only speculate. But while it poses problems for the application of his conceptual analysis to the contemporary world, it need not call in question the fundamental insight he has of a society as a concrete universal.

11. *GPR* §308.

X. 'Unhappy Consciousness' in Hegel

1. *The Phenomenology of Mind*. tr. J. B. Baillie, 2nd edition (London & New York: Allen & Unwin, 1955) 253.

2. Baillie, 255, 258, 263, and 265.

3. Baillie, 241.

4. *HGW*, 9.117–118; *Phen.*, 121; Baillie, 243–245.

5. G. W. F. Hegel, *Sämtliche Werke*, ed. Glockner (Stuttgart–Bad Canstatt, 1965) XVII, 76; *Hegel's Lectures on the History of Philosophy*, tr. E. S. Haldane and F. H. Simpson (London: Routledge and Kegan Paul, 1892) I 47.

6. Only the slave has appeared in the immediately preceding analysis. Universal mental cultivation presupposes the level of understanding, but it is not clear why the enlightened slave should appropriate it. The contingency of historical concreteness seems to have been introduced.

7. *Sämtliche Werke*, XVII, 76; *History of Philosophy*, I, 47.

8. He does not handle stoicism, skepticism and the unhappy consciousness in the section on self-consciousness. This poses interesting questions which deserve separate examination. How essential are these steps for attaining the level of reason? What is the systematic relation between the discussion in the *Encyclopedia* and that in the *Phenomenology*?

9. *Enc.* (*Philosophy of Mind*) §432, Addition. My italics.

10. Baillie, 241.

11. *Enc.* §435, Addition. Hegel stresses the universality of "all" in the next sentence: "Without having experienced the discipline which breaks self-will, no one becomes free, rational, and capable of command. To become free, to acquire the capacity for self-control, all nations must therefore undergo the severe discipline of subjection to a master."

12. *HGW*, 9.371; *Phen.*, 419f; Baillie, 699.

13. "Now finitude of the will characterizes the Orientals, because with them the will has not yet grasped itself as universal, for thought is not yet free for itself. Hence there can but be the relation of lord and slave, and in this despotic sphere fear constitutes the ruling category." From the *Lectures on the History of Philosophy* I. 96; *Sämtliche Werke*, XVII, 131. In the next paragraph Hegel refers to the oriental religious attitude as well.

14. *HGW*, 9.114; *Phen.*, 117f; Baillie, 238.

15. Psalm 111:10; Proverbs 1:7, 9:10. See also Job 28:28: "The fear of the Lord, that is wisdom." The expression is also used in §435 of the *Philosophy of Mind*. (Compare the final paragraph of chapter 4, where the passage of Job is found to be relevant to another Hegelian theme.)

16. *HGW*, 17.131–137; see G. W. F. Hegel, *Vorlesungen* (Hamburg: Meiner, 1985) 4a.58–66 and 356ff. The new edition makes it clear that the reference to the slave is in the lecture notes of 1821 but is not retained in either the lec-

tures of 1824 nor those of 1827. E. L. Fackenheim in *Encounters Between Judaism and Modern Philosophy* (New York: Basic Books, 1973) documents the inadequacy of Hegel's understanding of Judaism. "Abstract lordship" is found in Roman religion as it culminates in emperor worship, although Hegel makes no mention of slave-consciousness in this context. See *HGW*, 9.262–4; *Phen.*, 292–4; Baillie, 504–6, and *Vorlesungen*, 4a.584–6, 589ff; Hegel, *Lectures on the Philosophy of Religion*, ed. P. G. Hodgson (One-volume edition) (Berkeley: University of California Press, 1988) 381ff.

17. *HGW*, 9.261; *Phen.*, 290; Baillie, 502. My italics.

18. *HGW*, 9.239; *Phen.*, 264; Baillie, 459.

19. "When again [spirit] holds fast by the other abstract moment produced by analysis, the fact that its object is its own self become objective to itself—is its self-existence—then it is *Self-consciousness.*" *HGW* 9.239; *Phen.*, 264; Baillie, 459.

20. See the introduction to the *Phenomenology*, *HGW*, 9.53–62; *Phen.*, 46–57; Baillie, 131–145.

21. Both the master and the slave treat the other simply as a means to their own self-knowledge.

22. Similarly Hegel's comment in the *History of Philosophy*, cited above, that there can be no stoics today refers to the total context and not simply to the moment of individualistic self-concern.

23. Elsewhere, in "Virtue and the Course of the World," Hegel explores the motivation of the knight of virtue. And "Spirit in Self-estrangement" considers aspects of faith and culture embodied in the medieval world.

24. *HGW*, 9.122–131; *Phen.*, 126–138; Baillie, 251–267.

25. The reader is reminded that "eucharist" is derived from the Greek verb for "to give thanks."

26. Compare especially the analysis of consciousness in estrangement on *HGW*, 9.288; *Phen.*, 323; Baillie, 551.

27. *HGW*, 9.403; *Phen.*, 456f; Baillie, 755.

28. Kierkegaard presented a radical challenge to this presupposition in *Philosophical Fragments*.

29. *HGW*, 9.403; *Phen.*, 456f; Baillie, 755.

30. See the comment by E. R. Dodds, *Pagan and Christian in an Age of Anxiety* (Cambridge: Cambridge University Press, 1968) 3: "The evidence for them is chiefly inscriptional and inscriptions seldom tell us much about the underlying religious experience." The source used in the present discussion is Franz Cumont, *Oriental Religions in Roman Paganism* (New York: Dover, 1956), originally published in 1906.

31. Ibid., 56ff and 98.

32. Ibid., 96.

33. Ibid., 41, 39. See also the description of the taurobolium on p. 66.

34. Ibid., 40.

35. Ibid., 41.

36. Quoted in H. C. Warren, ed. *Buddhism in Translation* (New York: Atheneum, 1963) 333. This work, A. K. Coomaraswamy, *Buddha and the Gospel of Buddhism* (New York: Harper, 1964), and *The Buddhist Tradition in India, China and Japan*, ed. W. T. de Bary (New York: Vintage, 1972) are the sources used in this discussion.

The concentration on individual salvation and the refusal of the Buddha to answer questions concerning the cosmic order (see Warren, 117ff.) correspond to the isolated individualism of the section on self-consciousness. We might note as well that the age in which Siddartha Gautama was born was one of skepticism and doubt: "Siddatha experienced the intellectual and spiritual unrest of his age.... We know, for example, that many groups of wandering ascetics were engaged in the same quest, and that they were largely recruited from an intellectual and social aristocracy to whom the pretensions of Brahmanical priestcraft were no longer acceptable, and who were no less out of sympathy with the multitudinous cults of popular animism." (Coomaraswamy, 9–11).

37. de Bary, *The Buddhist Tradition*, 94.

38. "The knowledge of misery, O priests, the knowledge of the origin of misery, the knowledge of the cessation of misery, and the knowledge of the path leading to the cessation of misery, this, O priests, is called 'right belief'.

"The resolve to renounce sensual pleasures, the resolve to have malice towards none, and the resolve to harm no living creature, this, O priests, is called 'right resolve'." (Warren, 373)

39. "But by charity, goodness, restraint, and self-control man and woman alike can store up a well-hidden treasure which cannot be given to others and which robbers cannot steal." (de Bary, *The Buddhist Tradition*, 36) "Your majesty, he that is not free from passion experiences both the taste of that food and also passion due to that taste; while he who is free from passion experiences the taste of that food, but no passion due to that taste." (Warren, 421)

40. Warren, 374.

41. "The speaking of what has no sense or meaning" (*HGW*, 9.130; *Phen.*, 137; Baillie, 265) may find its embodiment in the Ceylonese monk reciting in Pali the virtually infinite permutations on the Buddha's counsel, or in the cryptic incomprehensibility of the Zen koan.

42. It is interesting to compare Hegel's somewhat inadequate discussion

of the cult of Buddhism in *Vorlesungen*, 4a.211–218 and 458–475; *Philosophy of Religion* (One-volume edition), 250–267.

43. E. R. Dodds draws a parallel between second and third century Rome and our day: "In calling it 'an Age of Anxiety' I have in mind both its material and its moral insecurity; the phrase was coined by my friend W. H. Auden, who applied it to our own time, I suppose with a similar dual reference." (E. R. Dodds, *Pagan and Christian*, 3) A passage in Cumont, written in 1906, sounds like a prophecy of the 1960s and 70s: "Let us suppose that in modern Europe the faithful had deserted the Christian churches to worship Allah or Brahma, to follow the precepts of Confucius or Buddha, or to adopt the maxims of Shinto; let us imagine a great confusion of all the races of the world in which Arabian mullahs, Chinese scholars, Japanese bonzes, Tibetan lamas and Hindu pundits would be preaching fatalism and predestination, ancestor worship and devotion to a deified sovereign, pessimism and deliverance through annihilation—a confusion in which all those priests would erect temples of exotic architecture in our cities and celebrate their disparate rites therein. Such a dream, which the future may perhaps realize, would offer a pretty accurate picture of the religious chaos in which the ancient world was struggling before the reign of Constantine." (196ff.)

44. The liberal assurance of immanent progress had given way to despair of ever attaining a just society by means of our present social structures and political constitutions.

45. My colleague, Michael Neumann, recently provided a trenchant analysis of the New Left movement of the 1960s and 70s. See *What's Left? Radical Politics and the Radical Psyche* (Peterborough: Broadview, 1987).

46. Baillie, 241.

XI. *God, Man, and Death in Hegel's* Phenomenology

1. A. Kojève, *Introduction*, 574; tr. J. J. Carpino, "The Idea of Death in the Philosophy of Hegel," in *Interpretation*, III (1973) 155.

2. *HGW*, 9.107f; *Phen.*, 109ff.

3. *HGW*, 9.110ff; *Phen.*, 113ff.

4. *HGW*, 9.112; *Phen.*, 115.

5. *HGW*, 9.114f; *Phen.*, 117ff.

6. *HGW*, 9.122ff; *Phen.*, 126ff. See Chapter 10 above.

7. In the discussion of pleasure and necessity (*HGW*, 9.201; *Phen.*, 220) death reappears as the impersonal, indifferent necessity that the individual consciousness experiences when it affirms its life by seeking only its own

pleasure. This experience of lifelessness marks the finitude of pleasure's abstraction from the total dynamic of life, and is therefore the first negation; but as *experienced* it has already been transcended. Therefore it becomes the second negation, which will lead on to the subsequent stage of "The Law of the Heart."

8. "Der Geist ist das *sittliche Leben* eines *Volks...*" *HGW*, 9.240 (Compare *Phen.*, 265.) In the twentieth century, *Volk* is better translated as "people" than as "nation." Until the eighteenth century, *sittliche* meant the characteristic ethos of a community or people. It would appear that this sense is in Hegel's mind more than the now current sense of "ethical" or "moral."

9. *HGW*, 9.241ff; *Phen.*, 267ff.

10. It may be misleading to see this as applying only to the Greek city-state. After citing examples of belief in life after death and of belief in communication between the living and the dead from Australia, Egypt, China, Rome, and America, Ernst Cassirer concludes: "All this shows in a clear and unmistakable manner that we have here come to a really universal, and irreducible and essential characteristic of primitive religion." *An Essay on Man* (New Haven: Yale, 1944) 85.

11. *HGW*, 9.246; *Phen.*, 272.

12. *HGW*, 9.255ff; *Phen.*, 284ff.

13. *HGW*, 9.275; *Phen.*, 307.

14. *HGW*, 9.293ff; *Phen.*, 329ff.

15. *HGW*, 9.316ff; *Phen.*, 355ff.

16. See the preface: *HGW*, 9.35; *Phen.*, 27.

17. See *HGW*, 17.131–137 and *Sämtliche Werke*, XVII 131; *History of Philosophy*, I 96.

18. *HGW*, 9.407f; *Phen.*, 462.

19. *HGW*, 9.409f; *Phen.*, 464ff.

20. *HGW*, 9.412f; *Phen.*, 467ff.

21. *HGW*, 9.414f; *Phen.*, 470ff.

22. *HGW*, 9.418f; *Phen.*, 475ff.

23. *HGW*, 9.422ff; *Phen.*, 479ff.

24. Two examples will suffice: "Although during the time of privation it seemed to me that I had utterly lost thee," wrote the mystic, Madame Guyon, "a certain deep support remained, though the soul knew it not: and she only became aware of that support by her subsequent total deprivation thereof."

(Cited in E. Underhill, *Mysticism* [New York: Meridian, 1957] 384). And Luther wrote in his *95 Theses*, "God works by contraries so that man feels himself to be lost in the very moment when he is on the point of being saved." (Cited in R. Bainton, *Here I Stand, a Life of Martin Luther* [New York: Mentor, 1959] 63). Luther, unlike the mystics, stops at a negative definition of Christian doctrine without progressing to a positive comprehension of the dynamic negativity.

25. Compare the final chapter of the larger *Logic*, "The Absolute Idea."

XII. The Syllogisms of Revealed Religion

1. *Enc.* (*Philosophy of Mind*) §§564–571; 1st edition §§465–471.

2. The following is a summary of a lengthier analysis of the syllogisms, to be found in my *On Hegel's Logic*, 158–192.

3. This transition of "becoming other," or "differing," is outlined in the discussion of becoming and alteration in Hegel's chapter on *Dasein*.

4. On the triple structure of reflection, see *On Hegel's Logic*, 67–72.

5. Aristotle's third figure.

XIII. Is Hegel a Christian?

1. The story can be found in G. K. Chesterton, *The Wisdom of Father Brown* (Harmondsworth: Penguin, 1970) 58–75.

2. J. N. Findlay, *Hegel: a Re-examination* (London: Allen and Unwin; New York: Humanities, 1958) 354.

3. W. Kaufmann, *Hegel: a Reinterpretation* (Garden City: Doubleday, 1966) 274.

4. R. Garaudy, *Pour connaître la Pensée de Hegel* (Paris: Bordas, 1966) 188.

5. Q. Lauer, *A Reading of Hegel's Phenomenology of Spirit* (New York: Fordham, 1978) 245.

6. C. Bruaire, *Logique et religion chrétienne dans la philosophie de Hegel* (Paris: du Seuil, 1964) 181.

7. M. Westphal, *History and Truth in Hegel's Phenomenology* (Atlantic Highlands: Humanities, 1979) 212.

8. See, for example, K. Marx, *Contribution to the Critique of Hegel's Philosophy of Right: Introduction*.

9. See in particular the various introductions to his Lectures on the Philosophy of Religion in which he discusses the concept of religion: *Vorlesungen* (Hamburg: Meiner, 1983) 3.95–108, 227–264 and 265–338. Compare the *Lectures on the Philosophy of Religion (One Volume Edition)* (Berkeley: California, 1988) 151–197.

10. *HGW*, 9.419; *Phen.*, 476. Some have suggested that the expression "I = I" was a reference to Fichte's use of that phrase in "First, absolutely unconditioned Principle" in the *Foundations of the entire Science of Knowledge* (*Fichtes Werke*, ed. I. H. Fichte [Berlin: Walter de Gruyter, 1971] I.91–101; ET *Fichte: Science of Knowledge*, ed. & tr. P. Heath & J. Lachs [New York: Appleton Century Crofts, 1970] 93–102.) This strikes me as a misreading. Fichte's "I = I" identifies an act of absolute self-positing, of confident self-affirmation; here, in contrast, Hegel is talking about the depth of the night. Fichte takes the assertion of self-identity as a beginning; Hegel talks about it as a despairing consequence. Fichte is exploring the rational, conceptual foundation of knowing; Hegel is talking about the feeling of the lack of substance. The difference in context indicates that the expression is being used in quite a different sense. If it is a reference to Fichte, it is used more ironically than directly.

11. *HGW*, 9.419; *Phen.*, 476.

12. "Holy Wisdom," cited by E. Underhill, *Mysticism* (New York: Meridian, 1957) 387.

13. *The Dark Night*, Book 2, Chapter 5, Paragraph 7; cited from *The Collected Works of St. John of the Cross*, tr. K. Kavanaugh & O. Rodriguez (Washington: ICS Publications, 1979) 337. My italics. It should also be noticed that St. John focuses on self-mortification as a preparatory stage. In other words, unhappy consciousness is an appropriate way of describing this phenomenon. T. M. Knox, as well, has suggested that Hegel appropriated this theme from St. John of the Cross: *Hegel's Aesthetics* (Oxford: Clarendon, 1975) II.824 n2.

14. "Leben," in Underhill, *Mysticism*, 412.

15. *The Dark Night*, Book 2, Chapter 9, Paragraph 1; *Collected Works*, 346.

16. I cite this from the *Evangelisches Kirchengesangbuch* (Karlsruhe, 1961), #73, although this version has amended the second line to read: "Gotts Sohn liegt todt." The original is cited in G. Lasson's edition of the *Vorlesungen über die Philosophie der Religion* (Hamburg: Meiner, 1966) II (*Die absolute Religion*) 158n1.
The hymn suggests that the death of God is the death on the cross. But that explanation is not sufficient. For Hegel, the death of God is not something reported in the tradition but personal feeling. The wording of the hymn ambiguously allows this interpretation when it talks of "grosse Not."

17. *HGW*, 9.354; *Phen.*, 399.

18. In the *Aesthetics* Hegel distinguishes the *truly* beautiful soul who acts

and is actual from the *morbid* beautiful soul of romantic irony. *Hegel's Aesthetics*, tr. T. M. Knox, I.67.

19. *HGW*, 9.352f; *Phen.*, 397.

20. *HGW*, 9.353; *Phen.*, 397f.

21. Cited from *Creeds of the Church*, ed. Leith (Richmond, Va.: John Knox Press, 1973) 121–2.

22. Ibid., 115.

23. Ibid., 122.

24. Ibid., 88.

25. *Enc.* §§564–571.

26. John 20:22.

27. See Chapter 12.

28. *The Will to Power*, §493; cited from F. Nietzsche, *Werke in Drei Bänden*, ed. H. Schlechta (Munich: Hanser, 1966) III, 844.

29. See Chapter 3.

30. Reported by Vahe Petrossian in the *Guardian Weekly* of August 26, 1990.

31. Compare I Corinthians 13.

INDEX